Winter's Grace

Winter's Grace

how anguish & intimacy transform the soul

K. WILLIAM KAUTZ

outskirtspress
DENVER, COLORADO

The opinions expressed in this manuscript are solely the opinions of the author and do not represent the opinions or thoughts of the publisher. The author has represented and warranted full ownership and/or legal right to publish all the materials in this book.

Winter's Grace
How Anguish & Intimacy Transform the Soul
All Rights Reserved.
Copyright © 2012 K. William Kautz
v4.0

Cover Image by Kay Marie

This book may not be reproduced, transmitted, or stored in whole or in part by any means, including graphic, electronic, or mechanical without the express written consent of the publisher except in the case of brief quotations embodied in critical articles and reviews.

Unless otherwise indicated, scripture quotations are from the Revised Standard Version of the Bible, © 1952 [2nd edition, 1971] by the Division of Christian Education of the National Council of the Churches of Christ in the United States of America. Used by permission. All rights reserved.

Scriptures marked NRSV are from the New Revised Standard Version Bible, copyright 1989, Division of Christian Education of the National Council of the Churches of Christ in the United States of America. Used by permission. All rights reserved.

Scriptures marked KJV are from the King James Version.

Scripture quotations marked NIV are taken from the Holy Bible, New International Version®, NIV®. Copyright © 1973, 1978, 1984, 2011 by Biblica, Inc. ™ Used by permission of Zondervan. All rights reserved worldwide. www.zondervan.com. The "NIV" and "New International Version" are trademarks registered in the United States Patent and Trademark Office by Biblica, Inc. ™

Scripture quotations from **THE MESSAGE.** Copyright © by Eugene H. Peterson 1993, 1994, 1995, 1996, 2000, 2001, 2002. Used by permission of NavPress Publishing Group.

Outskirts Press, Inc.
http://www.outskirtspress.com

ISBN: 978-1-4327-8657-1

Outskirts Press and the "OP" logo are trademarks belonging to Outskirts Press, Inc.

PRINTED IN THE UNITED STATES OF AMERICA

To Justin

Acknowledgements

On the second anniversary of my son's death, I received an email from an acquisitions editor named Kathleen Stephens. She had just stumbled on my website and a eulogy I had posted there and she suggested that I develop that eulogy into a book. Since that time, Kathleen has been a model of professionalism and compassion and without her encouragement, this book would never have become what it is. Her honesty and wisdom (when I needed a thump on the head), grounded me and matured me as a writer. It was Kathleen who reminded me that the highest form of communication is that which makes the deep and profound available to everyone. Every publisher needs an editor like Kathleen and I was blessed to have her expertise and friendship throughout this project.

I also want to express my gratitude to Jim and Susan Bajari who stood by me through my darkest hours and *believed* that I had something to offer. I don't think I will ever know anyone who better exemplifies a tender and sacrificial spirit than these two dear friends.

I am grateful as well for my dear friend Kay Marie Stefanoff who provided the image for the front cover. Kay is an award winning photographer and I'm honored to have the metaphoric beauty of that photograph grace the cover of this book.

Lastly, although my Mom is no longer with me, I want to acknowledge her amazing ability to encourage me and love me unconditionally – particularly as this book took shape. At ninety years old she still had a discerning mind and was always a willing sounding board as I wrestled with the contents of this book.

Table of Contents

Introduction i

Chapter 1: Eight Pounds of Silence 1

Chapter 2: Broken Cisterns 9
    Why the Orgasmic Lobster Roll Breakfast
    Can't Feed Our Need... 9
    Good Questions Asked in Anguish.. 19

Chapter 3: Coming to the End of Ourselves (Who Am I?) 23
    What's Love Got To Do With It? 23
    Why Intimacy Requires Failure and Hunger 28
    Hardwired Humanity... 36
    A Wormhole in the Cosmos 40

Chapter 4: Love, Chaos, and the Plans of God 47
    Freedom and Redemption... 49
    The Face of the Deep.. 50
    Restoration's Consuming Fire 54

Chapter 5: Finding Our Place on the Slippery Slope
(Why Am I Here?).. 57
    Healing and Purpose 58
    Doing Justice 61

Loving Mercy 67
Walking Humbly 70
Letting Go 73
The Empowering Paradox 74

Chapter 6: Till My Trophies at Last I Lay Down
(Where Am I Going?) 77
Performance and Grace 78
Grace and Peace 86

Chapter 7: Waking the Vision of Sleeping Dust 91

Endnotes 99

Introduction

There is something about anguish and intimacy that makes me think of tempestuous lovers. At first glance they seem mismatched and yet, somehow, they need each other. This is because the human cry for significance is often formulated with pain and then answered with a tenderness that can only belong to those who have been seared. That's why these two opposites are so bound to each other. Without comfort, there is no need for burning. Without burning, there is no need for comfort.

It's also curious that the magnetism between these two 'lovers' has inspired the arts as much as any other subject and whether the passion is expressed in poetry, painting, drama, or song, we are often startled by the way our deepest longings transcend the mediums that gives them voice. Although I enjoy writing and I sculpt and paint for a living, it is music (that thing that I do poorly) that has always transported and transfigured my soul more than any of the other arts. I wish I could play an instrument well enough to tug at the souls of others the way others have tugged at mine.

While emotional pain and spiritual joy have formed the wailing wall of every musical genre, I've often thought that it found its most humble expression in the temple of bluegrass music. I realize that's a very subjective statement and I'll own it as such, but when I hear the plaintive words and melodies of simple souls from the rural mountains of America, I am always struck by how their wisdom transcends everything and can silence the most learned voices. It is a genre whose melodies require us to acknowledge who we are and to stand in awe before something much bigger.

One song that yanked at my soul in particular is "Angel Band." It is simple and spiritually tender and it doesn't boast of any complicated theological concepts. It is just the honest cry of one who has suffered enough and is ready to meet God. Sometimes simple is also deep.

> *My latest sun is sinking fast,*
> *My race is nearly run;*
> *My strongest trials now are past,*
> *My triumph has begun*
>
> *Oh, come Angel Band*
> *Come and around me stand*
> *Oh bear me away on your snowy wings*
> *to my immortal home. . . .*[1]

I was raised in a part of America where bluegrass music was rarely heard. I didn't even know what it was until I was in my thirties. I think Emmylou Harris was the first person to captivate me with its beauty. I've since become intoxicated by the glory of its harmonies, the instrumental skills of its performers, the spiritual purity of its yearnings, and the honesty of its notions about life and love. But despite the astounding dexterity, speed, and soulfulness that the genre requires of its performers, the lyrics still manage to convey a timeless humility to its listeners, as if the music—even with all its beauty—could never be as fetching as the message it offers.

This, of course, isn't a book about music. But I felt like a musician when I wrote it. I've referred to a verse from "Angel Band" because after we suffer a loss, we all long to be transported somewhere—not to escape, but to understand . . . or to at least find peace. I felt like a musician because to write about such things requires more than just words. It requires a melody of transfiguration—something that reaches deep into our souls and asks us to not run away from our traumas, failures, and fears but to see them in a larger context and to be restored.

This book is written by someone who can't play the mandolin, the hammered dulcimer, or the pedal steel guitar. But I lost a child who loved me. I've seen anguish and desperation embraced by intimacy and joy as if they were engaged in some strange, romantic waltz. And I've been mesmerized by it. When such things happen to us, our hearts are like stringless instruments—offering their soulful sounds and hoping to bring some meaning to those who remain here with us. A songwriter writes words that people sing. I wanted to write words that sing to people. It's not really music, I know. It's still just words. But sometimes words can become flesh and dwell among us with a deep and redeeming grace.

1
Eight Pounds of Silence

My son was twenty-five years old when an avalanche swept him over a seventy foot cliff. That's him on the back cover—facing forward, upside down—flying wingless somewhere above Colorado. There were times when I questioned whether I could be happy again. I love him and miss him beyond words. But this isn't a book about grief. It's a book about *wonder*. Not the kind of wonder that asks "Why me?" but the kind that asks "Why do our souls hunger when our bodies are well fed?" I'll admit, I was tempted to throw a pity party for myself. But pity parties are boring and unpublishable and I'm hoping to accomplish something here. So let me tell you only briefly about the day Justin died, because it's such a human story and because I'd like to take you to a place of mystery and awe whose beauty may be, in the end, the reason for everything.

On the morning of January 5, 2007, my son and two of his buddies, Josh Smith and Joel Bettner, set off from their cabin in Wilson, Wyoming, for a day of backcountry skiing in the Tetons. They had scoped out a cliff named Fat Bastard on the previous day and Justin was eager to jump it as he had done many others. The three young men were each expert skiers who had competed with some of the best in that sport. Josh was a coach and former ski patroller and Joel had been on the ski team at the University of Colorado. Justin was an intense competitor. He would regularly do flips off of cliffs in the back country of Colorado and Wyoming and wherever else the powder was calling. He had received endorsements from several companies as a result of some incredible feats captured on film.

When they reached the top of Fat Bastard late that morning, Justin began to plan his descent. Josh and Joel had decided not to jump that day and so they watched from a few meters away as my son made two trial runs to the edge of the cliff. After studying the terrain, practicing his speed, and identifying his launching point, Justin began sidestepping up the slope to position himself for the final run. As he approached his starting point, the three young men heard a fracture in the underlying snow further up the mountain. The sound was followed immediately by a wall of hissing powder racing towards them from above. Josh and Joel had no option available to them other than pointing their skis towards the cliff and waiting for the inevitable. The next thing they knew, they were falling backwards down the sheer side of a rocky cliff surrounded on all sides by a cold, white terror.

Justin had almost positioned himself for the jump before the avalanche struck. As soon as he heard the fracture, he pointed his skis downhill and tried to outrun the cascading snow. Within seconds it overtook him and he was forced to launch in the wrong place. He sailed into the air above the cliff, and in the blink of an eye his fate was sealed. Instead of landing on a slope at the bottom that would have absorbed some of the impact and allowed him to ski away, he hit the base of the cliff at a place that was almost dead flat. He landed on his skis and his knees hit his chest with the power of a swinging baseball bat. Josh and Joel fell on their backs, partially buried but miraculously unharmed. They dug themselves out of the snow and raced to find my son. Two firefighters out for a ski that day arrived at the scene a few minutes later.

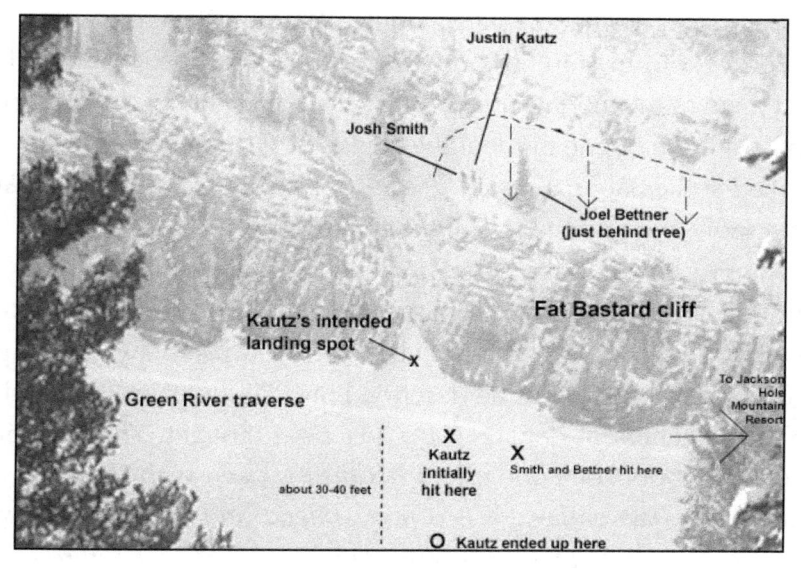

Photo and labels courtesy Thomas Gatehouse

    At first it looked like everything would be okay. My son's only visible injury was a rotated lower left leg. He had a strong pulse and was breathing normally. Justin was asked whether he felt any pain but he could only groan. He must have been in shock at that point. Someone called the Jackson Hole Mountain ski patrol for help, and within fifteen minutes the first patroller arrived with a toboggan. A few moments later, my son's vital signs began to drop rapidly. He stopped breathing and lost consciousness. The firefighters and friends started CPR and continued this for thirty minutes, but Justin died before he was even loaded onto the toboggan. He had bled out internally from massive injuries to his lungs and kidneys. A doctor from the resort's clinic pronounced him dead at the scene, and I lost a dear friend, a courageous advocate, and one of the great joys of my life. It was 12:30 in the afternoon.

    I received the news later that night as I was visiting with my mom, who lived next door to me. She was ninety years old at the time and Justin had always been a loving grandson to her. Whenever he would come home to Vermont he'd sit beside her on the sofa and open up his laptop to show her his skiing videos. At around 7 p.m., two police cars drove into my mother's driveway looking for me. I went out to greet them as my mom waited inside. The officers handed me a slip of paper with the phone number for the Jackson County Sheriff's office. I looked at the paper and said, "My son lives out there." They looked at me sadly and told me to call the number.

After rushing into the house, I called the sheriff and was informed that I had lost my son. What passed through my mind at that point was beyond words. When a priceless person is taken away in a split second, the thoughts can be described but not the pain. I remember the attractiveness of denial: *This can't be,* I thought. *The guy must be talking about someone else. I had just spoken with Justin on the phone a few days earlier. He is young, athletic, and full of life. He calls me every few days. It just isn't possible that I will never hear from him again. I invested twenty-five years into his life. There has to be some mistake. Somebody misidentified my son.*

But I also knew that no sheriff would deliver this message unless it was true. I just felt shock. I couldn't cry at first. I remember shaking. I went into my mom's living room and sat down. She entered the room a few minutes later and saw the grief on my face. "What's wrong?" she said. I couldn't answer. I just stared at her, wondering how to tell her and fearing what the news might do to her. When the words finally came out, we both broke down crying in each other's arms and I heard her say, "Why Justin? Why him? Why? Why? Why?"

Justin had been such a thoughtful, loving, mature person. Everybody respected and admired him. He had a strong faith and it showed in the way that he cared for people. Even though he was struggling financially like many other twenty-five year olds, he always gave ten percent of his earnings to someone less fortunate than himself. He had a social conscience and was especially devoted to a charity called Invisible Children, which cares for young people who had been forced into warfare in Uganda.[2] He had also advocated against the death penalty in America and had hoped to see it eliminated in his lifetime.

Three years earlier, his mom had left me after twenty-five years of marriage. She had fallen in love with someone else. Justin and I had many conversations then about grace and forgiveness and the struggle to understand things that are beyond us. At a time when I felt shamed and betrayed, he wrote to me:

> *Dad, I want you to know how grateful I am for the time we had together during these last three weeks. I'm honored to be the son of a man so honest, and with such a strong conscience in the midst of indescribable pain. You showed me a part of your soul when I was home and it was one of the most powerful experiences I've had. You showed me what being in love entails, and I pray that one day I will understand its depth. I definitely feel closer to understanding after our conversations. No one has shared that much of themselves with me before. Thank you, Dad. I will continue to pray in every free moment that healing will come. Thank you for being the most honorable man I know.*

When I was suffering, he knew exactly how to comfort.

When we lose someone we love dearly, we resist accepting it but we also understand the futility of that resistance. So we ask questions and look for answers and take whatever comfort there is. One of the sweetest letters I received after Justin died was from a young woman named Christy who had grown up with my son and continued a close relationship with our family. She attended three memorial services for Justin, including one that took place at the foot of Fat Bastard several days after he died. That cliff had now become a metaphor of life and death. Fat Bastard—what a fitting name for death. What a fitting name for the disappointments of life. Christy told me that several dozen young people lay on their backs in the snow looking up at the cliff and the clouds wafting through the vast Wyoming sky amid the grandeur of the Tetons. What a contrast that must have been between the intense grief and the awesome beauty of that place. She later sent me a card that said:

Justin's memorial service here was deeply touching on so many levels. He had a huge impact on people in Jackson. His life has been an incredible inspiration to me and all the people he knew. We went to see him at the funeral home on the day of the service. I broke down instantly and had a difficult time stopping the flow of tears. When I was finally able to stand up and look down at him, it was amazing. Will, he looked so beautiful and so handsome. There was a certain peace about his face. He lived more fully, with more zest, more passion, more motivation, more dedication, and more love than anyone I have ever known. When we were ending our time with him, Justin's friend Paul was standing next to me, proudly looking down at his dear friend. He said, "He lived well and I am so proud of him." So thank you Will, for raising a son who became such an incredible man. Please know that he lived life to the fullest and brought everyone around him up. . .

A few days before Justin died, I had been going through all the old family photos—looking at the faces of my four children and their mom as we all laughed and played and built a life together. I had bought a photo album and had planned on organizing all the pictures in chronological order. When the news came of Justin's death, there were dozens of photographs spread out on my bedroom floor. They remained there for weeks as the family tackled all the decisions that had to be made regarding the memorial service in Vermont and the funeral expenses and coordinating the visits from friends and extended family. One of the decisions that we made was to have Justin's cremated remains flown back home. I wanted to fly to Wyoming to get him, but at the time it was impossible.

As parents, we are accustomed to picking up our kids at school or church or at a friend's house. When they go off to college, we become familiar with train stations and airports and bus terminals. But nothing can ever prepare us for the day when we have to retrieve a child from the post office. The postmaster in my little town knew what the box was. She looked so sad. His ashes weighed just eight pounds.

I remember when Justin was an infant, I would take him in my arms and tell the world, "This is my son!" He was my first child. I was so proud. It was a new experience for me. Now, twenty-five years later, when I returned home from the post office, I sat down alone on my bedroom floor, amid all the smiling photos of a once happy but now broken family, and I took the bag of ashes out of the box and held his eight pounds of silence in my arms. I just wept and rocked him back and forth saying, "This is my son," all the while longing to make sense of the mystery of life and death and the movement of an infinite God through our own personal histories.

There is such a deep yearning in the human spirit to make sense of it all. Maybe we just want to bring order to chaos. Maybe we think that if we can understand the indecipherable, we can make ourselves secure. But sometimes our journey brings us to a place where we love the questions as much as their elusive answers, because the questions teach us humility and brokenness, which in turn lead us to a place we could otherwise never find.

2
Broken Cisterns

Why the Orgasmic Lobster Roll Breakfast Can't Feed Our Need

Many years ago, I was invited to visit some close friends on the south shore of Massachusetts. They owned a home in a quaint New England village where Greek Revival houses lined cobblestone streets and seafood restaurants overlooked a rocky coast. I could easily have made my home there. In autumn, every corner of the town belonged on a postcard. During my visit I was treated to breakfast at a local eatery. The place was popular among young people and was so full and noisy that a conversation was almost impossible. My friends assured me that the food was excellent so we found a table and I was instructed how to order. There were no menus. Instead, over fifty placards hung on the walls near the ceiling and on each placard was a breakfast option with a number beside it. If a customer wanted a simple omelet with bacon, he had only to scream "number 19!" to the waitress and hope that his order would be heard above the din.

As soon as I found my seat, I began to look over the choices. There were cranberry pancakes, exotic quiches with fresh veggies, waffles with homemade maple butter, and every conceivable breakfast a hungry traveler might want. I had almost made up my mind when my eyes fell on placard number 46. It said: *Orgasmic Lobster Roll Breakfast!*

Wow, I thought, *I'd like to have one of those.* But then I wondered, *How can it be? How can a cooked crustacean promise something like that?* I tried to picture it but I couldn't. I imagined that over the years, more than a few gullible patrons had gleefully screamed "number 46!" only to be disappointed when the boiled creature failed to deliver the goods. It made me think about salesmanship in general and how successful marketing plans often try to connect a product to some of the deepest longings of the human heart. A television commercial will promise relational intimacy if we just buy something as mundane as deodorant. Magazine advertisements tell us that freedom can be won with an airline ticket, honor can be earned with a Lexus, and a balanced life can be ours simply by eating a Nature Valley granola bar.

We can't walk through a subway, or turn on a radio, or read a newspaper, or listen to a campaign speech without being offered some variation of that orgasmic lobster roll breakfast. I think number 46 must be on sale in every corner of the world. Successful advertisers know that human beings *yearn,* and they know how to exploit that yearning. It's not that *everyone* is selling a lie. Right now, Jiffy Lube is promising a five dollar discount if I get my oil changed before the end of the month. It's an honest offer.

But sometimes a false promise that exploits our deepest longings succeeds in seducing us precisely because we *want* to be deceived. Usually when it happens, what we really want is *too hard* to get and so we convince ourselves that there is an easier way to reach our goal without ever having to struggle.

Here's an example: Most of us are communal creatures. But relationships of any kind are hard. Sometimes it's much easier to buy a car than it is to relate in a humble and sacrificial way towards someone we love. Even if that car costs a huge sum of money, it is often less painful to plunk down the cash or sign away our lives than to say "I'm sorry" to someone we care deeply about. Of course there's risk in signing a loan document. But we instinctively think that there's even more risk in admitting our humanity or our flaws to another person. So we substitute the joy of something deep and meaningful for the fleeting pleasure of something shallow, and then we deceive ourselves into thinking we're happy. It often works for a little while.

In the same way, it's not as hard to embrace religious rituals or regurgitate dogmas as it is to place our lives into the hands of an unpredictable God. Religion—even legalistic religion—can be far less complicated and arduous than a relationship. Religion is always predictable. There are formulas and well-choreographed procedures and we all know what to expect. It is calming. It is familiar. It can be as effortless as swallowing a bottle of liquor. But a relationship with a God who jars us out of our slumber is none of these things. When we hold well paying jobs and our reputations are secure and doctors tell us that we're healthy and our children make us proud, it's so much easier to secure ourselves on *those things* than to embrace a God who often asks us for intimacy by exposing the false foundations of everything that makes us feel safe and warm. It isn't until we lose something very dear to us, like a child or a spouse or a sense of safety, that we begin to realize that the trappings of religion are nothing more than an orgasmic lobster roll breakfast.

In the Bible, God is often portrayed as One who urges us to distinguish between religion and relationship. He stunned the pious by telling them that he really wasn't that impressed by their rituals and dogma. At times, he argued that humanity had actually *replaced him* with religion and he asked his people to think about why they would find cold, graceless orthodoxies to be more appealing than an intimate relationship with Someone who actually adored them.

> Be appalled, O heavens, at this, be shocked, be utterly desolate, says the LORD, for my people have committed two evils: they have forsaken me, the fountain of living waters, and hewed out cisterns for themselves, broken cisterns, that can hold no water.
> (Jer. 2:12–13)

I note this because if the reader has suffered some loss, it is important now—while your emotions are raw—not to allow yourself to be distracted by anything that promises easy answers or false comforts. There *is* comfort but be careful that you aren't tempted by a counterfeit that will leave you emptier at the end of your journey than when you first began. The comfort we long for is too deep and too profound to be *easy*. God often invites us to trust him as he takes us through a dark place—identified at times by intense anguish—so that the *real* intimacy and meaning we want can finally heal our souls.

I am reminded of what Rainer Maria Rilke says in *Letters to a Young Poet*:

> You are so young, so before all beginning, I want to beg you, as much as I can, to be patient toward all that is unsolved in your heart and to try to love the *questions themselves* like locked rooms and like books that are written in a very foreign tongue. Do not now seek the answers, which cannot be given you because you would not be able to live them. And the point is, to live everything. *Live* the questions now. Perhaps you will then gradually, without noticing it, live along some distant day into the answer.[3]

So how does it work? How do personal failures or heart-wrenching losses produce something positive in our lives? How can anguish and vulnerability transform us into people who are defined by humility, intimacy, selflessness, and even joy? How does God use sorrow and brokenness to identify and heal those wounds that we have been so careful to conceal *even from ourselves*?

My purpose in writing is to encourage readers to examine God's character and come to a clearer understanding of who we are, why we are here, and where we are going. The comfort will follow these things. Anguish has a way of driving us to these most basic questions and intimacy eventually provides the answers. Both can be very scary. Anguish and intimacy require much from us. It's not possible to go deeper in our understanding without embracing the mysteries and complexities of life that are often so disheartening. They are disheartening because they leave us feeling angry and confused and sometimes ashamed. So we avoid the mystery and give in, at times, to the seduction of simplistic answers and judgments.

The earliest book of the Bible dealt with this seduction. The book of Job tackled the problem of pain and evil as it came to a man who didn't deserve either. Job was a righteous man. He loved his family and provided for all their needs. He cared for the poor and was known for his compassion and sensitivity. He treated his workers fairly. Young men asked for his counsel, and his peers revered him. He acknowledged God in all that he did, and was blessed with health and wealth and children and honor.

But all that came to an abrupt end in just a few disastrous days. His crops were destroyed. His livestock were consumed by fire and plundering armies. His children were wiped out by a hurricane, and his body was overtaken by disease. All his wealth disintegrated and what remained of his former life was a wife who told him to "curse God and die" and a sorry collection of friends who said, "Job, you must have done something wrong."

When Job's friends first arrived at the scene, they were shocked by what they found. They couldn't bring themselves to say anything for seven days and seven nights. They simply sat with Job in silence. We can only wonder what was going through their minds. As men who cared for Job, they were distraught at seeing this once-thriving, revered man now reduced to a humiliated soul with boils all over his body.

But Job wasn't the only one being tormented. His friends had held to a belief that all of Job's wealth and honor were due to his righteous life. It was a theology that brought them much comfort. They had managed to inhabit a complex world while denying its complexity, and now the entire foundation of their sense of security was exposed as shallow and simplistic. How could it be that a righteous man should suffer? What does this say about God? Is God not powerful enough to redeem? Does he even care? What does it say about their own vulnerability? If their theology was wrong, then no one was safe—not even them. If a righteous man like Job could be brought to such a place of suffering, then what was next *for them*? Before they finally spoke, they must have wrestled with these things, and in the end chose to avoid the complexity by returning to a quaint, comforting lie.

Job must have some hidden sin, they thought. If he would only confess, they could feel safe again. Their theology would be intact and the illusion of their security would be complete. And so their sermons began. The reader of the oldest biblical book is treated to pages and pages of oratory offered by frightened little men who were desperate to bring order to chaos. The saddest thing about it was that they revered their theology more than their friend and more than God. They preferred to blame Job (as if he wasn't suffering enough) rather than acknowledge their total inability to codify the mind of an infinite God. Despite all of Job's subsequent protests, his friends continued to beg for a confession and they did so under the pretense of some divine authority.

We laugh at Job's friends and sometimes scorn them. But they are us. Every person who has ever lived could be rightly named Eliphaz the Temanite, Bildad the Shuhite, Zophar the Naamathite, and Elihu the Buzite. We all long for easy explanations and a sense of security. There have been times when we have preferred a pretty lie over an ugly truth. We have each, no doubt, forsaken personal and scholastic integrity in order to avoid the painful task of examining ourselves and the true reasons we hold to some system of thought.

I practiced law for ten years as a volunteer in Vermont's family court. Most of my cases involved domestic violence. One day I learned of a young girl who had been molested by someone she had trusted. While visiting her counselor one morning she was asked how things were going. "Everything is great," the child replied. The counselor didn't buy it. "Everything is fine? Are you sure?" "Yes," replied the girl, "as long as I don't wear my red dress."

In that child's mind, the responsibility for her pain had shifted to the clothes she had worn on the day of her abuse. She couldn't control an abuser but she could control her attire. What she feared was powerlessness in the face of danger, so she convinced herself that she had total authority over her own safety. All she had to do was wear the right clothes, she thought. We are like that little girl sometimes. We yearn for security and will do anything to achieve the illusion of it—even if it means clothing ourselves in something completely incapable of saving us.

Job didn't have that luxury because he had already lost everything. He was in the thick of it now. When disaster struck, he immediately saw the stupidity of his former confidence, and he cried out to God for a new theology—one that would explain the pain and vindicate him before his accusers. But God wouldn't give him what he wanted until he had given him something better. It was perhaps the best gift of all. It was a sense of wonder. It was an acknowledgment of mystery. It was humility. It was a broken and contrite heart. It was the beginning of wisdom. It was *awe*.

After thirty-seven chapters of sermons and protests, the writer of the book of Job tells us that God appeared to Job "from the eye of a violent storm" (Job 38:1, The Message) and began asking him dozens of unanswerable questions:

> "Where were you when I created the earth? . . . Who decided on its size? . . . Who came up with the blueprints and measurements? How was its foundation poured . . . ?"
>
> (Job 38:4–6, The Message)

> "Have you ever gotten to the true bottom of things, explored the labyrinthine caves of deep ocean? Do you know the first things about death? Do you have one clue regarding death's dark mysteries? . . . Do you know where Light comes from and where Darkness lives so you can take them by the hand and lead them home when they get lost?"
>
> (Job 38:16–20, The Message)

> "Are you going to haul me . . . into court and press charges? . . . Do you presume to tell me what I'm doing wrong? Are you calling me a sinner so you can be a saint?"
> (Job 40:2, 8, The Message)

Job had questioned the goodness and the power of God. He had decided that either God didn't care about the indignities he suffered, or that God was too weak to do anything about it. He wouldn't curse God, but neither would he honor him as just or sovereign. Job was too wounded and too angry to understand. So God questioned him further:

> "Can you pull in the sea beast, Leviathan, with a fly rod and stuff him in your creel? Can you lasso him with a rope, or snag him with an anchor? Will he beg you over and over for mercy or flatter you with flowery speech?"
> (Job 41:1–3, The Message)

> "If you so much as lay a hand on him, you won't live to tell the story. What hope would you have with such a creature? Why, one look at him would do you in!
> If you can't tame Leviathan, why do you think you can tame me?"
> (Job 41:8–9, The Message, v. 10, author's paraphrase)

Many more questions were posed to Job, and by the time God was done Job was undone. He could offer no response other than to say,

> "I spoke about things that I did not understand, things that were too beyond me to even know."
> (Job 42:3, author's paraphrase)

> "I admit I once lived by rumors of you; now I have it firsthand—from my own eyes and ears! I'm sorry—forgive me. . . I'll never again live on crusts of hearsay, crumbs of rumor."
> (Job 42:5–6, The Message)

Until we encounter God firsthand—an encounter that seems so often to be preceded by suffering and anguish, or a desperation that leads to an emotional, scholastic, and spiritual humility—all theology, good and bad, will be little more than the stale crusts of someone else's orthodoxy.

There was a time in my life when everything went perfectly. People told me that whatever I touched turned to gold. I enjoyed believing them. I relied heavily on my natural gifts, and for some reason never ran into any significant problem that would bring me to the end of myself. My children were adorable. My wife was faithful. My business was successful. There were people who told me that they patterned their lives after mine. It wasn't until I encountered the limits of my natural abilities, my powerlessness, and the inevitable loss of respect that always accompanies failure that I began to realize that I needed something or someone bigger than me. There is something fundamentally redemptive about anguish because there is simply no emotional need to question anything or delve deeper when we are comfortable.

In his book *The Problem of Pain,* C. S. Lewis writes:

> When Christianity says that God loves man, it means that God *loves* man: not that He has some "disinterested," because really indifferent, concern for our welfare, but that, in awful and surprising truth, we are the objects of His love. You asked for a loving God: you have one. The great spirit you so lightly invoked, the "lord of terrible aspect", is present: not a senile benevolence that drowsily wishes you to be happy in your own way, not the cold philanthropy of a conscientious magistrate, nor the care of a host who feels responsible for the comfort of his guests, but the consuming fire Himself . . . "[4]

God labors to make us whole—often through the dynamics of suffering. Of course, it is painful. Intimacy is never solely ecstatic.

More often than not, it is found in the arms of a loved one who is sobbing with us. Lewis writes further, "To ask that God's love should be content with us as we are is to ask that God should cease to be God."[5]

C. S. Lewis understood love in its most mature form. He understood that the love of God necessitates growth and maturity in us, as painful as such things are, and it doesn't stop at mere benevolence but rises to the level of a searing flame, burning off the dross and refining the gold. Sometimes, it is only after the experience of suffering that we are able to even know what we really want for our lives. Maturity does that. It cultivates a yearning for deeper things in a heart that once had no such yearnings. According to Lewis,

> Those divine demands which sound to our natural ears most like those of a despot and least like those of a lover, in fact marshal us where we should want to go if we knew what we wanted.[6]

My own anguish was used to redefine my calling and purpose in life after I delivered my son's eulogy (see Chapter 7, pp 91-99). I posted the eulogy on my business website, and after a short time the site began receiving three thousand hits each month. I suddenly began receiving emails from people who wanted to tell me about their own losses and encourage me to write more. People were actually saying that I had changed their lives and that they would never be the same again. I was left wondering how a dead son and a grieving father could influence so many people we had never known. I began to think about my life in ways that I had never considered before. My son's death was beginning to transform me and the lives of others as well, and as I heard from these people a new vision emerged that I would never have even imagined before Justin was taken.

One of the things I did was to follow the advice of my newfound internet friends. I began to write. Each weekend I sat on my bed with a laptop and poured out my soul until this book began to take shape. On the second anniversary of Justin's death, the book was nearly complete. I took the day off to reflect and pray and cry. Just as the hour approached that would mark the moment of my son's death, I called to God and asked that my loss would not be in vain but that he would do something redemptive in the lives of many other people through this tragedy. I imagined Justin pushing off in the snow one last time and sailing over that cliff. The thought of him hitting the bottom made me so distraught and emotionally spent and broken. I felt I had nothing left inside me to give. I had been lying on my bed for a few hours and after praying that prayer, I sat up and turned on my laptop computer. An e-mail had just been sent to me from another unknown person who had read Justin's eulogy. She told me that she was an acquisitions editor for a publishing house and wondered if I would be willing to write a book. It amazes me how we make plans but God writes the stories of our lives.

Good Questions Asked in Anguish

Through suffering, we come to grips with who we really are and we begin to catch glimpses of God's plan for us. In that sense, we are all like Job. He was forced out of the complacency he once knew. He wrestled with the injustice of his losses and the accusations of his friends. Eventually, he was driven to acknowledge his total inability to make sense of it all. He shook his fist at a rumored God—only to find him to be light years beyond the comfortable reflections of someone else's need for security. His experience raised reasonable questions. How do we find peace in an unpredictable world? How do we grapple with spiritual ideas when they are clouded by mysteries and distorted by pain? Why do the righteous suffer? Why do the wicked prosper? On what do we anchor our souls when the oceans are too deep to plumb? Is there any rhyme or reason to what God does? Is there a plan in the chaos? Is there wisdom in suffering? Is it really possible for us to find power in powerlessness? Would God pitch his tent on our slippery slope? Who *are* we to God? Why has he placed us here? Is our world merely an incubator for some future hope where all of our aching griefs will one day make sense? Where are we going? Some say we are just the products of a cosmic randomness—an unintended coincidence of nature. If so, by chance, we may or may not be valuable. According to this view, if we are worthy of something, it is at best temporary and inadvertent.

But Job discovered meaning in the mystery. God injected himself into history. He took an interest in Job's life even before Job's epiphany. *The suffering was evidence of that.* Job, in his lifetime, never was told what had happened behind the scenes that led up to his ordeal. God kept him in the dark about that. In God's economy, it wasn't important for Job to know. Other things were more important—things that couldn't be known without a desperate sense of wonder and awe. When Job encountered God—the person, not the rumor, he recognized that behind all the undecipherable questions was a loving Creator who took an interest in him and wanted him to draw near. That, in fact, was the reason for the suffering. What Job learned was that when we relinquish the *rumors* and finally encounter the *person* of God firsthand, we discover something about ourselves as well. We are "fearfully and wonderfully made" by a Creator who intended each of us for a specific purpose (Ps. 139:14, KJV). This Creator endowed us with a uniqueness and a moral character that makes intimacy with him possible (despite the mystery and unpredictability of God) and that intimacy is more satisfying than the health and wealth and places of honor that Job had once enjoyed.

If someone were to ask me, "Will, what do you want more—intimacy with Someone who adores you, or places of honor?" my answer would be a very human, "Yes." I want both. I want intimacy with God, but I don't want to be slandered. I don't want to be mischaracterized. I don't want to be shamed, like Job, by false accusations. When I do my best, I don't want to be subjected to ridicule. When I identify some problem, I don't want to be punished, dismissed, devalued, or disowned.

But what if intimacy with God sometimes guarantees betrayal, abandonment, ridicule, and loss? What if there are times when it's not possible to walk with God in a fallen world without being crucified or stoned? What if the only honor in seeking God is dishonor among those who don't? What if the world is filled with alienated souls who are so terrified by the idea that they are in need of redemption and restoration that they can't even look at themselves or bear the thought that someone else might know this, their darkest secret? What if Job's friends are everywhere? Maybe the only thing left to say then is "I want intimacy with God, and I want that intimacy to produce a tenderness in me towards those who are so wounded, frightened, and damaged that they can't honor anyone or anything at all." But that is humanly impossible. *Without a consuming fire, it is beyond our grasp.* How can anyone acquire such tenderness or sustain such an attitude for long without that fire?

Bingo.

What Job discovered was a paradox. His powerlessness was the very thing that brought him to a place of power. It brought him to the throne of God. None of us could ever transcend our blinding biases or our inability to love the unlovely or our presumptuous confidences in our own strength until we are first rendered powerless. Only then, in that desperate place, will we have any reason to let go of former things and allow God to reveal himself and transform our lives for the better.

Certainly, when we accept by faith that God desires us, it is just another leap of faith to presume that the Creator also has a plan for us and that he wishes to superintend our search for meaning as we place ourselves in his loving arms and seek the meaning that only he can give:

> "Live in me. Make your home in me just as I do in you. In the same way that a branch can't bear grapes by itself but only by being joined to the vine, you can't bear fruit unless you are joined with me. I am the Vine, you are the branches. When you're joined with me and I with you, the relation intimate and organic, the harvest is sure to be abundant. . . I've loved you the way my Father has loved me. Make yourselves at home in my love. . . I've

told you these things for a purpose: that my joy might be your joy, and your joy wholly mature."

(John 15:4-11, The Message)

But all this requires a huge leap of faith whose authenticity is unknowable and even unimaginable until the leaper has actually leapt. And even then our own subjectivity is continually suspect.

3
Coming to the End of Ourselves (Who Am I?)

It's time to take a journey deep into the human soul. Our only supplies will be courage, integrity, and something to quench our thirst. We'll barter for a wide-angle lens near the end of the trip, but for now we don't need one. Since broken cisterns are useless, our burdens will be light. Our sustenance along the way will be fluid and living rather than stagnant and dead. It must be this way because we are beginning a great exploration to the far limits of our power and understanding. Some of this will be painful. It is a journey for the brokenhearted—not for the faint hearted. We have spent so much of our lives cultivating a pretense of strength but now we will look at our *weakness*—the very thing that we have dreaded and denied—so that we can arrive at a place where we finally embrace the magnificent beauty of our own inadequacies.

What's Love Got To Do With It?

Many years ago, I wrote a Valentine's Day story for someone I loved. I wanted to say something about our vulnerability and how two solitary people might complete each other if they could only find a way to speak about their frailties with honesty and grace. To do this, I personified truth and love as if they were two very different kinds of strangers who were curious about each other and who, despite their trepidation, knew they couldn't live apart. I'm still convinced after many years that true intimacy with anyone is only possible when humility and tenderness are present. This is how my story went.

> Some time ago, Truth and Love met by chance on a sleepy moonlit night. At first there was hesitation as they stood several yards apart—each viewing the other as a stranger in their land. But gradually they moved closer. A conversation began, and after only an hour they found themselves as separate and inseparable as freedom and unity.
>
> Truth proposed to meet Love again, and Love agreed—suggesting a time on the following night. They arrived at the appointed hour dressed in their finest clothes. Truth came with his firm structure of rationality and fact, while Love appeared with her graceful compassion and flowing mercy. Never was there a stranger contrast of compatibles—such that a passerby might wonder at it and yet predict the inevitable romance.
>
> And so the romance began, day after day and night after night, until all other social values—humility, justice, integrity, and peace—were hardly surprised when a wedding was announced. The day arrived with impatience, but finally Truth stood at the altar with a coattail tux and a splendid bow tie. Love, appearing in a glorious brocade gown, stepped slowly down the aisle to meet her waiting mate. With promises made and ceremony complete, the two then left the bustle of friends and family and hid themselves away from all but themselves.
>
> That evening, Truth determined to experience risk with all its frightful joy. He shed his coattails and bow tie and stripped himself before Love and took on the appearance of one who saw the inadequacy of pure reason. For the first time in his life he

found redemption in his weakness and scorned the pretense of his power. Said Truth to Love: "You have always seen me clothed in the praises of scholars, now I feel ashamed and vulnerable and incomplete without you."

Love expressed surprise, but as she slipped her lacy veil from her head and her gown fell to the floor, she also felt the same sense of inadequacy. "You have always seen me arrayed in the poetry of sentimentality," she said, "but now, I too feel ashamed and vulnerable and incomplete without you."

In a moment the two were one—making passionate love through the night. Their kisses sent a hush through stagnant ivy halls while musicians, cinematographers, and playwrights were silenced by their moans. Later that year, a child was born and they called the infant Wisdom, because wisdom always happens at the mating of Truth and Love. Without Love, Truth is just a geek professor who never learned to relate to a single soul. Without Truth, Love is merely gushy—unable by itself to understand why something is broken, or to redeem that which is lost, or heal a throbbing grief. In some mysterious way, the nudity of these two lovers revealed a paradox that clothed them in a glory that no Parisian designer could duplicate, no scientist define, no dreamer describe.

So what if you and I were matchmakers? What if we carried a hope that on some sleepy moonlit night Truth and Love might meet? Would such a meeting really be by chance, or must it be determined ... by us? And even if by chance, must we then become superfluous? Perhaps the encounter is rare in a world of empty extremes and unsatisfied hunger. Perhaps its rarity proves coincidence rather than intent. Unless, intent is itself rare and our own responsibilities too often shunned. I think the latter is most likely true, for the moonlight shines in our hearts tonight, where strangers could meet yards apart, separate and inseparable, and you and I must place them there.[7]

Justin always lost interest in dating whenever ski season began. I would call him up and ask him about his love life and he'd say, "Dad, it's ski season" (as if nothing more needed to be said). But during his senior year in college he began dating a young woman named Tammy who didn't enjoy competing with something as inanimate as snow for my son's affection. So she asked him what his priorities were, and apparently the question caused Justin to do some thinking.

A short while later, Tammy was in a serious snowboarding accident that landed her in a hospital for several weeks. My son went to visit her. Tammy later told me that she was embarrassed when he arrived. She was in a lot of pain and hadn't been able to take a shower or wash her hair for days. She had no make up on, and soon after Justin walked into the room and sat on her bed she became so nauseated by her pain that she got sick all over the sheets. Justin began to clean things up and they talked. He told her he had never seen her so beautiful. The beauty he spoke of went far beyond physicality. All the masks were off. There was no sense in furthering any pretenses. Tammy was too exhausted to even try. Justin found that attractive. I know him well enough, and the circumstances that he grew up in, that I'm pretty sure he longed for a woman who could let her guard down and show herself for who she really was. There is something so gorgeous and safe about such a woman. Justin was interested in more than externals and knew them to have only a temporary appeal. His visit to Tammy's hospital bed allowed him to discover a new definition of beauty—one that allowed an intimacy of the soul.

Intimacy is achieved by *being real* within a context of graciousness. Often, that requires a certain amount of anguish, because we have to come to the end of ourselves and our pretenses before we can ever be honest with another person. But it takes a great deal of personal strength to be real with someone. In their book, *Groups: Process and Practice*, Marianne Schneider Corey and Gerald Corey, write:

> Power and honesty are closely related. In our view powerful people are the ones who can show themselves. Although they

COMING TO THE END OF OURSELVES (WHO AM I?) | 27

may be frightened by certain qualities within themselves, the fear doesn't keep them from examining these qualities. Powerful people recognize and accept their weaknesses and don't expend energy concealing them from themselves and others. In contrast, powerless people need very much to defend themselves against self-knowledge. They often act as if they are afraid that their vulnerabilities will be discovered.[8]

One of the great mysteries of humility is that by shedding all the pretenses that we formerly used to feel safe, we actually become more desirable. People are drawn to a *person*—not to a pretense. If someone's desire for "safety" is stronger than her desire for honesty and intimacy, then she may end up spending decades with people who will eventually say, "I never knew you." Henri Nouwen describes this dynamic as it applies to leadership, but it is also true of all relationships:

> What makes the temptation of power so seemingly irresistible? Maybe it is that power offers an easy substitute for the hard task of love. It seems easier to be God than to love God, easier to control people than to love people, easier to own life than to love life. Jesus asks, "Do you love me?" We ask, "Can I sit at your right hand and your left hand in your kingdom?" One thing is clear to me: the temptation of power is greatest when intimacy is a threat. Much . . . leadership is exercised by people who do not know how to develop healthy, intimate relationship and have opted for power and control instead.[9]

So what does it mean to be a part of an authentic community where we are able to be *real* rather than phony, *deep* rather than shallow, *stimulating* rather than boring, *full* rather than empty? What does it mean to take off our masks and shed the pretense of invincibility or flawlessness and confess our weaknesses to others in an atmosphere of grace? By baring our souls, we encourage other authentic, healthy people to do the same. We create a culture of humility and grace where it is safe to be real despite our flaws. It is hard to do this when the people around us are frail and wounded and unable to trust. But we all hunger for grace and instinctively feel lost without it.

The loneliest kind of loneliness isn't the kind that we feel when we are alone. *It is the kind that we feel when we are treated as worthless in the company of others.* It is rare to find another soul who will love us the way we were created to be loved. A true, authentic intimacy requires the vulnerability of two people who are willing to bare their souls to one another and receive the joy of being fully known and fully accepted.

There is a verb used in the original language of the Bible that describes this kind of intimacy. The word is translated *to know* but the Hebrew meaning is much deeper than its English counterpart. When the Bible describes a cheapened sexual relationship between two people, which is purely mechanical and devoid of any emotional or spiritual connectedness, it often uses the phrase *he went into her.* But when the Bible describes a deep, tender, selfless intimacy between two people who are each giving their entire soul to the other person, it uses the verb *to know*. One can't have true intimacy unless there is "knowing" and this requires more than the vulnerability of baring one's body. It requires the frightening joy of baring our entire soul—with all of its inadequacies—and being desired anyway by another who is doing the same for us. *It is this frightening joy that God has created us for and we cannot be who we are meant to be without it.*

Why Intimacy Requires Failure and Hunger

I once belonged to a church where one could hear beautiful sermons on grace. But over time I realized that the leadership of that church had difficulty actually creating a culture of compassion or a sense of safety. There was an eagerness in the pastor to imagine the worst about people and to condemn. Perhaps the most visible example of this involved a member of the church who suffered a brain injury in a car accident. I'm not a neurologist but it was clear to almost everyone that some trauma to the man's brain had damaged his ability to function in socially appropriate ways. He would send out strange e-mails and engage in awkward behaviors. The minister chose to see it as a moral or spiritual problem rather than a neurological one, and after trying unsuccessfully to reason with the man he decided that this handicapped individual should be disciplined. An announcement was made to the entire congregation that the man was not welcome back in the church unless he repented.

I couldn't help wondering what would happen to me if I became injured and couldn't think rationally anymore? Would I be discarded too? If a man could be disciplined for a brain injury, could anyone really be safe? Could anyone expect to be loved unconditionally? Maybe the reason this injured man was in our lives wasn't so that we could teach him how to behave properly. Maybe *we* were the ones who needed to learn something. Maybe he was there so his presence would *teach us* how to live gracious and compassionate lives.

I also realized that if I was wondering these things, there were probably others asking the same questions and that it might be too dangerous to ask them out loud. It really didn't matter how beautiful the sermons were, the real message that was sent in that church was that it's not safe to be human and vulnerable and real and damaged. In such a context, everyone needs a mask. To avoid shame, one must feign perfection even though the entire enterprise is a joke. *Authentic intimacy requires a different way of living.* The masks come off and the walls fall down wherever honesty is followed by tenderness and mercy. *Without such a love, we are all broken beyond repair.*

In the gospel of Luke, a story is told about a woman who enters the home of a Pharisee named Simon to anoint Jesus' feet with oil. She is a woman with a damaged reputation. Although she is scorned by those present, she bravely enters the house to express gratitude to Jesus and to nurture an intimacy with someone who had welcomed her as she was. She is emotionally vulnerable and in tears—having opened herself up to the ridicule of others—but she enters anyway. Simon seems bothered by her presence but says nothing. So Jesus speaks to him:

"Simon, I have something to tell you . . . Two men were in debt to a banker. One owed five hundred silver pieces, the other fifty. Neither of them could pay up, and so the banker canceled both debts. Which of the two would be more grateful?" Simon answered, "I suppose the one who was forgiven the most." Then turning to the woman, but speaking to Simon, he said, "Do you see this woman? I came to your home; you provided no water for my feet, but she rained tears on my feet and dried them with her hair. You gave me no greeting, but from the time I arrived she hasn't quit kissing my feet. You provided nothing for freshening up, but she has soothed my feet with perfume. Impressive, isn't it? She was forgiven many, many sins, and is so very, very grateful. If the forgiveness is minimal, the gratitude is minimal." Then he spoke to her: "I forgive your sins." That set the dinner guests talking behind his back: "Who does he think he is, forgiving sins!" He ignored them and said to the woman, "Your faith has saved you. Go in peace." (Luke 7:40–50, The Message)

What startles me about this passage is the obvious contrast between the woman's humility and the Pharisee's self-righteousness. The irony of seeing an irreligious woman demonstrating the highest ideal of religion (a broken and contrite heart), and the orthodox Pharisees demonstrating a complete unawareness of their own depravity (spiritual pride) is painful to us. In each of these characters we see the self-inflicted torture of the human condition. These are *our* characters in this story. We have played the roles of the Pharisee and the sinner many times. When we fail, we weep and ask for mercy. When we succeed, we pridefully wonder why others haven't. We have each played the part of the failed sinner and the sneering goody-goody.

Notice the relationship between humility and intimacy in this story. The Pharisees are polite—after all, Jesus has been invited to Simon's home. They are also keeping their opinions of the woman to themselves—at least there is no verbal condemnation. But their silent hubris fills the room and is so awkward that it can't be ignored.

The result is a distinctive social and spiritual disconnect between the Pharisees and their guests (both wanted and unwanted).

The woman, on the other hand, is as connected to Jesus as anyone ever could be. The spiritual union between this woman and her Savior is defined by gratitude, humility, intimacy, and forgiveness. *It doesn't get any better than this.* A scorned failure in the eyes of the religious, she has achieved the highest level of spirituality. She has not done this by donning the dogmas of the haughty, but by collapsing at the feet of Christ, emptied of any presumptuous confidence and overflowing with a passionate adoration of one who adores her as well. *This is what we were meant for.* Perfection isn't possible. Intimacy is. No matter how terrifying it is, if we are ever to find fulfillment in any relationship *or meaning in any anguish*, we must first bare our souls and our weaknesses to another and say, "This is who I am in all my glory and all my shame and grief—please love me anyway."

Remember, we are on a journey deep into the human soul. Our only supplies are courage, integrity, and the water of life. This woman in the gospel story had all three. Everyone else saw her as a failure, but she was the only one who succeeded, because her brokenness had brought her to a fountain of life where her thirst was quenched and her wounds finally healed.

Twelve years ago, one of my daughters brought home a new friend. She was a sweet girl with great big beautiful dark brown eyes and two little sisters. As my family grew to know these girls, we learned that each had been subjected to an enormous amount of harm. Two of the three had been molested. Each sister had a different father and the fathers were not in their daughter's lives at all. I remember the first time I took them to a nearby lake. I asked the youngest girl, who must have been about three years old, if she wanted to play on a swing beside the lake. Her face lit up as I set her on the seat. I gave her a push and she sang, "Higher Daddy! Higher!" I hadn't spent more than a half hour with her and already she had adopted me. When I picked her up she threw her arms around my neck and clung to me as if she would never let go. At the same time, some of my children were entering their teenage years and the contrast between their desire for independence and these three sisters' longing for connectedness seemed stark and painful to me.

During this time, I would often recall the joys of being a young father. My children had always been eager to play with me. We would build Legos and hunt imaginary grizzly bears and make up mischievous stories at bedtime. My daughters used to argue over who would come with me on my business trips. I felt desired. It was work being a young dad—waking up in the middle of the night to change a diaper or comfort a crying child—but it was also fulfilling because there were always plenty of hugs and the gratitude was obvious.

But raising teenagers was another matter. It was easy to feel like a failure. A parent may go ten years or more without ever receiving a single word of affirmation. During the teenage years, it's not uncommon for a mom or a dad to feel like a car running on empty. When our definitions of justice conflict with those of an adolescent, there's the inevitable anger, resentment, and misunderstanding that leaves everyone feeling demonized. Setting boundaries for our children within a culture that encourages a sense of entitlement and a lack of respect can also be emotionally debilitating. One woman wrote to me recently and said that whenever she tries to connect to her teenage son, she is made to feel like a "complete moron."

What strikes me about the three fatherless girls I took to the lake is that their pain and their sense of abandonment gave them a better understanding of their need for a daddy than an adolescent who is defined by ingratitude or hubris. *Trauma does that.* It makes us aware of our deepest needs. The three girls never pretended to be more than they were. They never denied their need. They never feigned strength. They were emotionally engaged rather than emotionally detached. They were not ashamed to ask for love. *Their transparency made them absolutely adorable.*

Put these ideas on a back burner and bear with me while I share some thoughts on cats. I admit to knowing very little about cats. I know that there are tiger cats and tabby cats and Siamese cats and some cats don't have tails. But it always seemed to me that there were really only two kinds of cats: stray cats and house cats. Stray cats purr like a diesel engine and rub affectionately against your legs. If you give them a little milk they will adore you forever, or at least until they become house cats. House cats owe their lives to you but they don't know it. They might have known it once, but they forgot. They act annoyed at your presence. Give them some food and watch the ingratitude. Give them a home and they'll wonder why you haven't cleaned their litter box. *The most annoying thing about cats is that their nature is so similar to ours.* What is it that causes us to take for granted every good thing we've ever received? What causes us to lose our sense of wonder and awe over a beauty that should keep us mesmerized forever?

Each one of us knows what it's like to *be* a house cat and what it's like to *have* a house cat. We've been taken for granted and we've taken others for granted. There are times when we've felt so abandoned and forsaken that we could easily relate to a fatherless child sitting on a swing, yearning for intimacy with an unknown "dad" and screaming at the top of her lungs, "Higher Daddy! Higher!" We now know what it's like to sense that something redemptive and awesome has been missing from our lives. But perhaps what we *don't* know is how to find such redemption. We hear about a young woman scorned by society and tortured by her past who finally meets someone who validates her and honors her and adores her and so she pours out her gratitude at his feet and achieves the intimacy that she had always longed for. We hear about a three-year-old girl throwing her arms around a stranger who is willing to return the affection, but it rarely dawns on us as adults to do the same. That is, to throw our grateful arms around One who is a stranger to us now because we have wandered so far off, but who longs to redeem us and call us his own, if only we would come to the end of ourselves.

The point is we can't be aware of our hunger when we are full of ourselves. We feel hunger only when we know we are empty. It's the hunger and the anguish that drives us to ask the most important questions in life. What really matters? What really satisfies us? Why am I so empty? Where can I go to quench this thirst?

One of the most wondrous experiences a human being can have is to stand dumbfounded and mesmerized before some awe-inspiring mystery for which there is no explanation. A favorite movie of mine captures this experience beautifully. K-PAX (Universal Studios, 2001) is about a man who is both a visitor from another solar system and a patient in a New York psychiatric hospital. Throughout the movie, the viewer is left wondering who or what the man really is. Kevin Spacey brilliantly portrays Prot, the visitor who manages to mystically identify with the frailty and immeasurable worth of each broken soul he meets.

A crucial scene is set at a planetarium where Prot and his psychiatrist meet with numerous academics—each holding a PhD in astrophysics. Prot is asked to use a light pad to plot the orbital pattern of his planet around twin stars in the constellation Lyra. He begins revealing things that no human being could possibly know. As the story unfolds, we see cynicism melt into awe as Prot renders all the academics speechless.

There is something going on in this scene that has no rational explanation. A computer transposes Prot's drawings and mathematical formulas onto the planetarium's ceiling, and as his claims are verified a stunned look comes over everyone's faces. Silence and wonder fill the room. The psychiatrist, convinced that Prot is nothing more than a delusional patient asks, "What's going on?" No one has an answer. Prot puts down his pen and calmly inquires whether his calculations help explain the perturbations that these astrophysicists have been seeing in the rotation pattern of their binary star. More silence. *It is a silence filled with the ecstasy of bewilderment.* Everyone in the room has come face to face with the stunning beauty of the unknown and it dwarfs them. Finally, the most venerable scientist slowly asks: "How . . . how could you know this?"

I'm convinced that God wants to bring us to a place like this. He wants to bring us to the boundaries of our own understanding so that we can see something much bigger than us—not to shame us but to humble us (like Job). Because until that happens, we will be too stuck on ourselves to ever really know who we are in this universe. This is because *humility and truth are so interconnected that you can't separate the two without killing them both*. If we are ever to find our deepest meaning in the intimacy that we have been created for, then our only hope is through a broken heart that is screaming for wisdom and purpose.

But what about truth? How do we even *know* what it is? How do we even attempt to answer a question that is both the inquiry of an idealist and the sneer of a cynic? Sometimes we just get in the way of our own quests for knowledge. The idealist is often too naive and gullible and the cynic too suspicious to embrace certain spiritual ideas. This is why we need a healthy understanding of who we are before we can ever move beyond ourselves.

If an infinite God is *seeking us out* and wants to be in relation with us, we first have to understand that we are unable to get close to him on our own strength or through our own "wisdom." We are subjective. He is too far above us. He is too unlike us. He is in fact wholly different from anything we know. We don't even speak his language. He would have to speak ours. It would require something on God's part to make the relationship possible. We don't inhabit a high and holy place. We are children of the dust. We can't tame God. But when God approaches us and tells us *that very thing*—reminding us of our utter dependence on him for wisdom and understanding—and we are able to grasp at least *that truth*, something of the eternal enters us. Embracing truth requires brokenness and humility. It requires an understanding of our own limitations and a desire for something more—something far beyond ourselves.

I once heard a lifeguard offer some advice on how to save a drowning man. He suggested that one should wait until the man has completely exhausted himself and is ready to drop below the waves before any attempt is made to bring him to safety. If the drowning man is thrashing about hysterically, it is impossible to reason with him or offer any help. God is something like a lifeguard. He waits until we have come to the end of ourselves before revealing himself, because until we are thoroughly spent and no longer clinging to our own understanding we are unable to even know our need.

I remember the idealism of my youth and the presumptuous confidence I once had in my own abilities. I remember what began as an honest desire to love everyone and to work for peace during a time of war ended in my hating anyone who disagreed with my political views. I also recall the first time I glimpsed my own hypocrisy and realized that my very best efforts resulted in failure and shame. But it was a glorious failure because after all the thrashing I was able to come to the end of myself. I was ready to be rescued.

This is what happened to Job as well. He had spent years thinking that he had tamed Leviathan—that monster of the deep unknown. He had spent most of his life blissfully unaware of how stale, inadequate, and unsatisfying his "crusts of hearsay" were. It took a crisis to change that. Job had to be jolted out of his comfort zone with all its spiritual lethargy before he could ever contrast his "crumbs of rumor" with the astonishing revelations that God ultimately offered (Job 42:6, The Message).

Hardwired Humanity

So far I have used personal stories to illustrate ideas, because we all relate better to real people than to scholastic concepts. But indulge me for a moment as I shift from a personal to an historical look into the human condition, because it will reveal something important about us. It may be that humanity has been hardwired with certain vulnerabilities so that we can learn something about humility and be transformed.

Some of the most basic questions we could ever ask are, Do we need God or can we find our way without him? Can we arrive at the truth about who we are and why we are here, solely on our own strength and understanding? Are we basically good or do we need a Redeemer? These were the great questions of the secular Enlightenment and every one of us sooner or later has to face them. One side of the debate speaks of a fallen humanity in need of redemption and the other side champions the notion that humanity can save itself. The Enlightenment placed its faith in reason and objectivity and believed that all of our problems could one day be solved by the inevitable progress of rational, educated, objective human beings. To the Enlightenment, the mind was the ultimate messiah.

This optimism in human progress has expressed itself in many ways. When Adam Smith, the father of capitalism, published *The Wealth of Nations* in 1776, he acknowledged human failure in the form of greed and self-interest, but he saw it as only a minor problem. He believed that humanity was basically good and its self-interest could actually be the engine of enterprise that would elevate society to new levels. If, after all, an enterprising inventor could patent his designs and profit from them, then all of society would benefit. Self-interest was seen as something that was beneficial to all and the destructiveness of human greed and arrogance was downplayed by this new optimism.

As history unfolded two startling inconsistencies of the secular Enlightenment became obvious. First, the very movement that proclaimed humanity to be basically good and in no need of redemption also declared that "power corrupts and absolute power corrupts absolutely." *But if humanity is basically good, why would its power be so corrupting?* Second, the economic freedom that was cherished and promoted for the benefit of society also fathered a class of unchecked industrialists whose avarice and indifference towards the poor produced an environment where children labored for long hours in unsafe factories and where industrial toxins were dumped into rivers and lakes. Adam Smith's theory never predicted the radically destructive qualities of human greed. It only extolled the importance of rewarding creativity and inventiveness.

Within one hundred years the "progress of history and the perfectibility of man," which was a fundamental tenet of the Enlightenment, was now defined by a demoralizing sense of social and spiritual alienation. Hopelessness and despair gave birth to its alcoholic children, and adolescents who had lost limbs in factories were now being tossed away like barrels of industrial waste. Bordellos offered their small comfort and the line between morality and immorality became so blurred that each powerless person was seen by the captains of industry as someone who could be prostituted for the sake of a profit. Charles Reade spoke of the complete vulnerability of the poor at this time and wrote satirically about capitalism's insistence that no government should intervene: "'Every man for himself and God for us all!' said the elephant as he danced among the chickens."[10] When we minimize the destructiveness of human pride, bad things happen. When we embrace a naive optimism that ignores human limitations, we set ourselves up for failure.

In Germany, Karl Marx suggested yet another economic theory that, though enormously sympathetic to the poor, made the same mistake about human nature. Marxism suggested that humanity can save itself by the economic structures of socialism. To some, Marx became the new messiah and evil was seen as residing not in individuals but in systems and institutions. A new utopian vision emerged. It suggested that if we just change the structure of society, humanity will become suddenly virtuous. The secular Enlightenment had fathered yet another baseless optimism and even a quick glance behind the iron curtain could reveal how "virtuous" humanity became under such a utopian nightmare.

Czeslaw Milosz wrote in *The Captive Mind* how important it was for the Communist Party to draw people's attention away from any talk of human nature. Such talk exposed the Achilles heel of Marxism. It has always been the nature of dysfunctional humanity to avoid and deny its fundamental problem:

> Why does a good Communist, without any apparent reason, suddenly put a pistol to his head? Why does he escape abroad?... People who flee from the people's democracies usually give as

their chief motive the fact that life in these countries is psychically unbearable. They stammer out their efforts to explain: "The dreadful sadness of life over there . . ."

To forestall doubt, the Party fights any tendency to delve into the depths of a human being, especially in literature and art. Whoever reflects on "man" in general, on his inner needs and longings, is accused of bourgeois sentimentality. Nothing must ever go beyond the description of man's behavior as a member of a social group. . . . He is a social monkey. *What is not expressed does not exist*. Therefore if one forbids men to explore the depths of human nature, one destroys in them the urge to make such explorations; and the depths in themselves slowly become unreal.[11]

Milosz writes further:

Russian revolutionists discovered what they claimed were effectual means of mastering the forces of History. They proclaimed they had found the panacea for the ills of society. But History itself repays them in jeers.[12]

So the twentieth century began with a revolution in Russia and World War I. The West was stunned by the horrors of both. Waves of humanity could now be decimated in minutes. Life had never been so cheap. The early gulags of the Soviet Union and the trenches of the First World War offered up their human sacrifices as if to a new god. The secular Enlightenment had given the world a faith in the progress of history and the perfectibility of man and the spiritual bankruptcy of that faith was now being witnessed by everyone. Poison gas and the first use of aerial warfare seemed to define and promote the anonymity of one's opponents, and the advances of modern weaponry seduced the world with its power.

A worldwide depression followed. Its devastation in Europe and the Treaty of Versailles with all its retribution and vindictiveness combined to produce astronomical inflation in Germany. A million marks could barely buy a loaf of bread. It was time for a new "messiah." Suddenly, one of the most educated and enlightened nations on earth was now being governed by a madman building the most technologically advanced war machine in history. Hitler began another world war, and the unsubstantiated optimism of the secular Enlightenment was exposed for what it truly was. By the time the Second World War was over, sixty million people had perished, and within a few decades there was hardly a liberal mind that clung to the former optimism. Now the intelligentsia were moving closer and closer to complete moral skepticism. Only the most naive would still preach optimism. Everyone else understood. *It is not possible to poke our heads into an oven at Auschwitz and preach the progress of history and the perfectibility of humankind.*

A Wormhole in the Cosmos

So the question is raised: Do we need something greater than our own minds to move beyond the mess we've created? At no point in human history has the question been more pressing. We are now capable of complete self-destruction. The Enlightenment's optimism has been replaced by self-loathing because the brutality of the twentieth century destroyed the very basis of its hope. Secular scholarship has swung from naive idealism to a paralyzing cynicism, and the pedigree of this cynicism is anger, disappointment, and shame. So, like the drowning man, we have come to the end of ourselves. Our pridefulness and our self-confidence brought us to a place of exhaustion and failure. What the twentieth century did was to strip humanity naked and force us to acknowledge the utter stupidity of any confidence in our own power. Despite all the technology and all the advances, the fundamental problem of sin and self-acquittal remains. We are faced with an intellectual acknowledgment of the real problem (which the Enlightenment dismissed), but no secular solution. The legacy of the Enlightenment has been a moral vacuum that has, according to Abraham Joshua Heschel, promoted *"a spiritual homicide [through] the systematic liquidation of man as a person."*[13]

But the secular mind doesn't have a monopoly on pride. The most haughty forms of religion have also advocated a terribly naive optimism that claims objectivity can be ours simply by embracing the doctrines of a particular denomination. Amazingly, this view also de-emphasizes the problem of pride. It sees human subjectivity as little more than a fallen tree on the path of life. It views our blinding biases as just a minor nuisance that one must step over or walk around in order to discover the truth. And yet, Martin Luther King's famous statement about Sunday mornings being the most segregated hour in America stands as a sharp indictment on any view that turns human bias into a minor nuisance. *There is no significant acknowledgment of sacrifice or struggle in this religious optimism—as if the deepest intimacy is possible without anguish.* There is little emphasis on the awful pain or the intense battle that we must endure before we can ever breath the words, "He must increase and I must decrease" (John 3:30, KJV). It is a system that isolates people into closed subcultures so that any unpleasant truth or experience can be avoided and then it promises that this is the way to arrive at wisdom. The biblical concept of a broken and contrite heart is light years away from such naivete. Os Guinness, in his book *Time for Truth,* describes the dishonesty of those who are caught up in their own religious subjectivism as nothing more than an escape from scholastic integrity:

> Retreating into the fortress of personal experience, they can pull up the drawbridge of faith and feel impregnable to reason. But for all of them the outcome is a sickly faith deprived of the rude vigor of truth.[14]

Human pride and subjectivity is *not* a minor nuisance on the pathway of life. It is the Himalayas. It is the Mariana Trench. It is Donner Pass in a blizzard. It is the Fat Bastard of every spiritual pilgrimage.

But the secular pessimists are right in one respect. There is no way that we can make it across the abyss on our own strength. It's too vast and too deep. There is a kind of sad humility in secular pessimism now that is absent in lifeless religion. So the journey brings us either to a dead end, or it brings us to a spiritual wormhole in the cosmos that can transport us to a place—light years away—that would otherwise be impossible to find. *That wormhole is a broken and contrite heart*. Either we thrash about with a mindless sense of invincibility and eventually perish, or we collapse into the arms of a waiting Redeemer.

I believe God is calling you to let go of something. It might be a red dress. It might be a trust fund. It might be the emotional wall you've built around yourself. It might be an idolatrous love of some dogma that has become more important to you than God himself. It might be a condescending view towards some race or people. It might be the rage you continue to feel years after you were shamed and humiliated. It might be a graceless fundamentalism. It might be a proud and cynical atheism. It might be a kooky cult. It might be a debilitating hopelessness. The wormhole is still there. As long as you can breath, it will be there—waiting for you to loosen your white-knuckled grip on something that can never save you. Who are you? What defines you? *Why has it left you empty?*

The act of letting go is an act of humility. Releasing our grip on that false security is an acknowledgment of where our ultimate hope resides. Once this happens and the wormhole is entered we are essentially saying that our myopic opinions have lost their allure. They have now been replaced by a yearning for God, whatever the cost.

Think about the nature of true genius. It is something that is fundamentally dissatisfied with the status quo. It thinks outside the box. There is a word that describes this kind of thinking. The word is *iconoclasm*. It was originally used to describe the act of destroying religious icons because they were thought to be idolatrous. But the word has taken on a much deeper meaning. The iconoclast is someone who questions myths. True genius is inherently iconoclastic because it destroys conventional beliefs that can't do what they promise. It is not *eager* like some rebellious adolescent for whom rebellion itself is the only goal, but it is *willing* to shatter myths that don't make sense. It refuses to accept conventional wisdom because that wisdom has failed to explain some deeper reality, failed to heal some diseased body, failed to answer some persistent grief.

The iconoclasts of every scholastic discipline long to know what at first seems unknowable, and upon reaching that goal they expose the inadequacies of the prevailing wisdom. Iconoclasm, *like intimacy* requires us to bare our souls and risk exposing ourselves as mere human beings with no monopoly on the truth, no claim to omniscience, no complete freedom from our own contextual subjectivity, no perfect thinking. Without humility, there are no paradigm shifts. We cannot be faithful to the truth without understanding that there are too many unanswered questions and too many flaws in our own systems and that we are each sometimes driven by what we *want* rather than what is *true*. When we say, "I believe in God," aren't we really saying, "I *want* to believe in God"? When we say, "I'm an atheist," aren't we really saying, "I don't *want* to believe in God"? When we say, "I'm an agnostic," aren't we really saying, "I don't even *want to know* if there's a God"? What we *want* has nothing to do with the truth. If God exists, he does so independent of our own tempting wills.

People of faith are often described as content—as if their long quest has concluded and their hearts fully satisfied. But nothing could be further from the truth. If someone is satisfied, something is wrong. If the acquisition of truth is hindered by our wills, must we not then *sacrifice something* to get it? How far are we willing to go to grow and discover and mature? Are we willing to give up a false sense of security and risk being exposed as frail, vulnerable creatures who at times don't have a clue?

Now think about the iconoclasm of God. Think about the myths he has shattered.

> "You have heard that it was said, 'You shall love your neighbor and hate your enemy,' But I say to you, Love your enemies and pray for those who persecute you . . ."
>
> (Matt. 5:43–44)

God spoke to an upside-down world and gave us a vision of what it might look like if it was right-side up. He said, in effect, "What you call holy, I call profane. What you call normal, I call dysfunctional. What you call logical, I call nonsense." When the religious thought God was pleased with the mere form of religion, God inserted a radical notion into human history. Worship in the absence of justice is a detestable scandal:

> Take away from me the noise of your songs; to the melody of your harps I will not listen. But let justice roll down like waters, and righteousness like an ever-flowing stream."
>
> (Amos 5:23–24)

When humanity was impressed with scholarship, wealth, and military might, God spoke through Jeremiah and suggested that intimacy with one's Creator trumped the things that infatuate us most:

> "Let not the wise man glory in his wisdom, let not the mighty man glory in his might, let not the rich man glory in his riches; but let him who glories glory in this, that he understands and knows me, that I am the LORD who practices steadfast love, justice, and righteousness in the earth; for in these things I delight."
>
> (Jer. 9:23–24)

A. J. Heschel reminds us that when the world idolized power, an *omnipotent* God declared the *impotency* of brute, physical force: "Not by might shall a man prevail" (1 Sam. 2:9). Those who put their trust in their own power will be left embarrassed: "The nations shall see and be ashamed of all their might; they shall lay their hands on their mouths . . ." (Micah 7:16).

Before all else, we were created for intimacy with God. At the most foundational level, it is who we are and what we were meant to be. It is also why we are empty without him.

Edward Lorenz, a professor at MIT, wrestled with the tension between determinism and free will in his book *The Essence of Chaos* and drew some strength from a scientific premise. He said, "Let our premise be that we should believe what is true even if it hurts, rather than what is false, even if it makes us happy."[15]

This premise of a mathematician is essentially the call to discipleship. Jesus said, "If anyone would come after me, he must deny himself and take up his cross and follow me" (Matt. 16:24, NIV). But there is a paradox attached to the call. The cross, like the searing fire, at first glance is unappealing. It may refine our gold and melt our dross, but the pain repulses us. We may hesitate as we examine the choices, but we understand that mysteriously we can find no lasting joy outside of the loving arms of this Consuming Fire. So we offer ourselves, naked and aware of our inadequacies. The wormhole has a price but it is not shame. Indeed, the only shame is in not letting go of our baseless self-confidence.

The way of the Cross is permeated with paradox. It is a fierce and violent peace. By weakness we arrive at power. Through surrender we achieve victory. With poverty we become rich. *Because of our vulnerability we are made secure.* By laying down our lives we are saved. Through servanthood we find freedom. In humility we are glorified. We burden ourselves with this cross and become strangely unburdened. Even by all this "foolishness," we arrive at wisdom.

But who on earth can drink this cup? Despite its sweetness, it seems too bitter. So we enter our own personal Gethsemane. It is theological. It is social. It is economic. It is scientific. It is political. It is sexual. It is racial. It is every area of our lives and we struggle with the choices. We have grown to love our myopic opinions, and we draw close to the abyss of our own self-acquittal. We wince. We shudder. "Oh God, if it be possible, remove this cup from me" (see Mark 16:36). We sweat blood.

But when we lay down our lives, they become deep and full of meaning.

4
Love, Chaos, and the Plans of God

In the biblical book of Genesis a story is told about a boy named Joseph who was given a finely woven coat by a father who favored him over his brothers. Joseph's brothers eventually became so jealous and angry that they sold him into slavery to some traders bound for Egypt and then told their father that Joseph had been killed by wild animals. Joseph was seventeen years old at the time and spent the next thirteen years as a slave in Egypt.

Some of that time was spent suffering in prison and being victimized by false accusations. But some extraordinary things happened and one day Joseph found himself standing before an Egyptian Pharaoh who was upset about some dreams he was having. Joseph interpreted the visions and told Pharaoh that there would be seven years of affluence followed by seven years of famine in the land. He advised Pharaoh to store up grain and food during the good years so that the people would not starve during the famine years. Pharaoh was impressed. After consulting with his advisors, the King of Egypt put Joseph in charge of the whole project. It was an extremely important position—similar to that of a prime minister in today's world. At the age of thirty, Joseph went from being a slave to being one of the most powerful men in Egypt.

God had a plan for Joseph. The purpose wasn't to make Joseph a slave and it wasn't to make him a prime minister. The purpose went far beyond the horror and the splendor of those two positions. From a purely human perspective, it would be easy to focus on the humiliation and the glory of Joseph's status or the events that led up to those things. But there was a bigger picture.

As humans, we are inclined to view the events of our lives with a telephoto lens rather than a wide-angle lens. It would be easy for me, for instance, to focus on the death of my son and conclude nihilistically, "That's the end of it. I had Justin for twenty-five years and now I don't. Life stinks and nothing makes sense." In fact that's what often happens when tragedy strikes. We say, "Where is God?" and we zoom in on the real pain rather than the equally real movement of a loving God in our own personal histories.

It would have been easy for Joseph to turn bitter over the betrayal of his brothers and the apparent absence of a just God. But Joseph knew that if he was to stay grounded through the ordeal of slavery he would have to focus on the big picture. To Joseph, God was bigger than Joseph's brothers. He also knew that God's plan, no matter how painful, was to accomplish something restorative and redemptive in the lives of ordinary people.

When the famine years came to the land of Egypt and Palestine, Joseph's brothers, who were in Canaan at the time, began to go hungry so their father sent them to Egypt for food. Word had gotten out that there were storehouses of grain there. So the brothers arrived in the court of the prime minister and didn't recognize Joseph because he was now thirty years old and arrayed in the splendor of royal garments. But Joseph recognized his brothers immediately. When he saw them asking for food, he couldn't compose himself and left the room to weep alone. He had suffered for years because of what these brothers had done to him. He also now had complete power over them. He could order their execution. But he stayed focused on God and not on the evil done to him.

After a series of events, Joseph revealed himself to his brothers and asked about his father. The brothers thought they were as good as dead. But Joseph wept and hugged them and forgave them and uttered a famous line that's been repeated countless times by faithful people for forty centuries since: *"You meant evil against me; but God meant it for good"* (Gen. 50:20). Joseph had been brought by God, through his sufferings, to a place where he wouldn't focus on the wrong done to him or the pain of his life. Instead, he was focused on what God was doing and how God could take the cruelty of slavery and use it to set in motion a series of events that would ultimately save his family from starvation.

I believe that God can take something as ugly as a betrayal, as terrifying as a malignant tumor, or as heart-wrenching as the death of a child and do something redemptive with it. We see things in such a subjective way, but sometimes there is truth that is way beyond us. I am putting my faith in Someone who is bigger than me and bigger than an avalanche, and I am trusting that the ending of this story will be beautiful. I know I will see my son again and our time here will seem so short compared to eternity. In the meantime, we are here for a reason and I keep my eyes focused on the power of God to heal and restore and to use this tragedy to amaze me with a plan I never envisioned and to do whatever work in me that needs doing.

Freedom and Redemption

Freedom requires us to keep our focus. If we lose sight of the redemptive workings of God, we either become enslaved to cynicism or we suffer through an endless bondage of grief. I could focus on the fracturing of snow above my son's slope. I could also focus on the inexperience of youth and the reckless risks that young people take sometimes. Those things are true, but they are not the only truth.

The greater truth is that God uses even tragedy to accomplish something redemptive in the lives of the people he adores. He can take the apparent flukes of nature, the mistakes of others, and *the pain we feel* and like a loving father at some future time he can astound us with the full wisdom of his design. In the meantime, he uses adversity to draw us close to him. That's why we were created.

I don't think we can ever find ourselves, our freedom, or our ultimate purpose in life without first finding the Lover of our souls. It's not about the pain and it's not about religion. It's about being drawn closer to Someone who adores us and wants to liberate us. When Joseph was sold into slavery he must have been furious. There is no way he could have known what the ending of the story would be or how miraculously God would work in everyone's lives. But he trusted God to make it right and God didn't let him down.

The Face of the Deep

In the past few decades physicists and mathematicians have begun playing with a new science called chaos theory. One of the things that this theory examines is how order can arise out of apparent randomness or chaos. Computers can plot certain equations using millions of random calculations and the result on a monitor will be incredibly gorgeous patterns of art that reveal deeper and deeper levels of beauty and intricacy. A designed splendor appears even when numbers are randomly inserted into the equation. It may look like chaos at first, but when we delve deeper, we see it's more.

Before powerful computers were programmed to graph such equations, it was difficult if not impossible for us to reconcile the truth of a determined design with the truth of randomness and freedom. Indeed, almost every discipline including theology, psychology, sociology, biology, physics, and history has debated this tension. With the discovery of orderly patterns flowing out of apparent disorder, we have an example of how randomness and chaos may exist side by side with the plans of God and are not necessarily contradictory.

I believe our lives are like chaos theory. We are unable to predict the future. There are too many variables and too many unknowns. Millions of decisions are made by untold numbers of people and any or all of these decisions can profoundly impact our lives. A single event can shake our foundations until our illusions of security become like a dissipating mist. Everywhere we look we see haphazardness, serendipity, and chaos. And yet there is also the miraculous splendor of a determined outcome that bears witness to the plans of a loving God. If a computer can reveal the awesome beauty hidden behind a veil of randomness, how much more so can the Author of Creation? And if he adores you as his child, then every misery must be subject to his transforming grace.

Imagine you have an enemy who wants you dead. Imagine this enemy is extremely powerful and well-equipped to do tremendous harm. Now imagine that you have a friend who is proficient in the martial arts, and knows how to turn that enemy's power against itself. Imagine the force of an adversary's blows being harnessed by your friend to defeat this enemy. Every cruel intention and every vicious attack is directed back against the adversary so that even though your life is in constant danger, you are always protected. There is peril and safety, chaos and order, adversity and devotion—all at the same time.

You may not have to imagine this scenario—you may be living it now. You feel pain, powerlessness, and confusion. Your fear compels you to focus on the enemy and not the friend. Your circumstances may seem overwhelming. Maybe you are questioning your own worth. Maybe your life is in danger. Maybe you are wondering if you can hold on much longer and whether you even have anything to hold on to.

Throughout your whole ordeal, there are the lies. They begin at first as a whisper and then rise to a hateful sneer and then finally a raging torrent of venom:

You are worthless. You have failed. Your mistakes are unforgivable and the mistakes of others are your fault as well. You will never be loved. You will never receive grace. You will never amount to anything. You will never make sense of this horror. Let me destroy you. It's for your own good.

This enemy is as powerful with his words as he is with his deeds. You have the freedom to throw in the towel and give up. You also have the freedom to say,

> *I will not believe these lies. I will not succumb. I have an undefeated advocate. My Maker adores me. I am desirable. I am the apple of his eye. He hovered over the face of the deep and brought order out of complete chaos. He turned a slave boy into a prime minister. He fed the hungry in a time of famine. He redeemed his people from oppression. He exalts those of low degree. He put the haughty in their place. He is the voice of the voiceless, the power of the powerless, the defense of the defenseless. He has called me by name and made me his own. He triumphed over a grave and because of his victory, I will not be defeated.*

I recently met a woman who runs a funeral home in York, Pennsylvania. She has offered her services free of charge to many poor people in that working-class town who have lost children to drugs, violent crime, and untreated illnesses. Her love for humanity has given her many opportunities to share her faith with those who are in crisis. She and I spoke about the suffering that a family goes through after the sudden death of a loved one. I told her how surprised I was that after losing my son people seemed to value my advice and opinions more than before I had suffered the loss. She said, "It's because you're still standing, Will. So many people crumble under the weight of it all, and by simply functioning after a terrible loss we demonstrate a strength that people desire."

Those who are still standing after experiencing such misery often have a clear and tender understanding of the character and intentions of God. It is the kind of understanding that can heal a broken soul. It begins with the removal of the telephoto lens so that we can catch a glimpse of the bigger picture. It takes the focus off of the trauma *not by denying it* or removing it from the big picture but by placing that trauma into the larger context of a divine plan. It's not about slavery or famine or death. It's about redemption and purpose. It's about a sovereign God who governs the haphazard and rectifies evil—not by disallowing it, but by turning it against itself and transforming us miraculously in the process.

As we are being transformed we begin to see and accept God's calling for us. Mysteriously, the Lover of our souls incorporates our pain, our freedom, and our faithfulness into his designs. Think about it. What if God's best plan for our lives isn't activated unless we believe in his plan? What if our misery has no purpose unless we have faith that it does? What if Joseph's slavery would have no meaning unless he trusted God to act? What if Justin's death has no value unless I believe that God will use it? What if writing this book will have no redemptive power unless I know in my heart that God is orchestrating something transformational by it?

If these things are true, we determine far more than our helplessness might suggest. God's Spirit might blow where it wills, but our faith can become a partner and participant in that mysterious movement.

Once we begin to see the intentional and loving movement of God in our seemingly disordered and sometimes uncontrollable lives, we begin to realize that the opposite of freedom is pride. Indeed, as Abraham Joshua Heschel once wrote in *The Prophets:*

> The opposite of freedom is . . . hardness of heart. Freedom is not a natural disposition, but God's precious gift to man. Those in whom viciousness becomes second nature, those in whom brutality is linked with haughtiness, forfeit their ability and therefore their right to receive that gift. Hardening of the heart is the suspension of freedom. Sin becomes compulsory and self-destructive. Guilt and punishment become one.[16]

When we choose to walk away from the mystery of freedom—from the God who is sovereign over all things—we defeat ourselves and become enslaved to cynicism, rage, self-pity, and hatred. And these in turn give rise to deeper and deeper levels of bondage—often manifested in the form of an addiction to something that can never satisfy our hunger or heal our wounds. *Liberty without righteousness is slavery.*

After listening to the sermons of Dr. Martin Luther King, Jr., one is often forced to ask, Who is really in bondage? The slave or the master? Aren't they both? Isn't the slavery of the master so profoundly destructive precisely because he is completely unaware of his own bondage? He has ears that can't hear because he is deaf to the cries of the oppressed. He has eyes that can't see because he is blind to his own self-destruction.

Restoration's Consuming Fire

John Newton was a ship captain in the mid-1700s. He could sail wherever he wanted. When he took the helm he was the master of his own destiny. But what did he do with that freedom? He sailed for Africa. He bartered for human flesh and filled his gutted ship with the writhing misery of black humanity—shackled beside its own vomit in the belly of his beast. It was Captain Newton's ship. No one could tell him otherwise. He had the power. He had the wealth. What more could he want? The open seas afforded him the freedom to sail anywhere he chose, but he knew that there was one place he was not free to go as long as he clung to his power and his wealth and the means by which he secured them. He saw that he wasn't free at all. He was chained to the misery of others.

When a storm overtook him and his life was in peril, all his wealth, power, and freedom amounted to nothing. *"What does it profit a man to gain the whole world and forfeit his life?"* (Mark 8:36). On May 10, 1748, he called to God for help for the first time in his adult life. The turbulent seas were calmed and his life was saved and transformed. He left the slave trade and wrote a song. Actually, he wrote many songs but one stands out among all the rest:

> *Amazing grace! how sweet the sound*
> *That saved a wretch like me!*
> *I once was lost, but now am found,*
> *Was blind, but now I see.*

*'Twas grace that taught my heart to fear,
And grace my fears relieved;
How precious did that grace appear,
The hour I first believed!*

*Through many dangers, toils and snares,
I have already come;
'Twas grace that brought me safe thus far,
And grace will lead me home.*[17]

True freedom can never be defined apart from *humility*. We become empowered when we humble ourselves. That power can deliver us from the agony of any loss and even the terror of examining ourselves, because paradoxically it leads us to a place of safety. It leads us to grace. It leads us to redemption. But this safety, grace, and redemption comes to us through a Consuming Fire. It isn't an easy safety. It isn't a cheap grace. The redemption may be priceless but it comes with the cost of discipleship. Other things must be burned away before we can ever be restored. But once we find grace, the disappointments of life find their meaning even as we hurt. Without it we are slaves—unable to even discern our lack of discernment and trapped in a hopeless spiral of despair.

> But this is the one to whom I will look, to the humble and contrite in spirit . . .
>
> (Isa. 66:2b, NRSV)

> For thus says the high and lofty One who inhabits eternity, whose name is Holy: "I dwell in the high and holy place, and also with him who is of a contrite and humble spirit. . ."
>
> (Isa. 57:15)

5
Finding Our Place on the Slippery Slope (Why Am I Here?)

He has shown you, O man, what is good; and what does the LORD require of you but to do justice, and to love kindness, and to walk humbly with your God. (Mic. 6:8)

When I was in college, I met a young man working in the dish room who was affectionately known as Earl the Pearl. My friends and I never knew his last name—he was just a quiet, deep-thinking, solitary guy who wrote short stories and stayed to himself a lot. I think he wanted to be a hermit and a recluse and since those were also my vocational goals at the time, I decided to hang with him. I know that makes no sense, but I was young.

One day as we were talking about the spirituality of the counterculture he told me about the time he drove a VW beetle across the country. Somewhere in the middle of Arizona or New Mexico he picked up a longhaired hitchhiker who needed a ride through the desert to some small town on the other side. Earl agreed to drive the distance and they set off into the scorching wilderness. They drove for hours, passing tumbleweeds and sagebrush—all the while being blasted by the monotony of the miserable heat. Finally, a town appeared and when they pulled into the sleepy little place, the hitchhiker asked Earl to drop him off at the first corner. Earl pulled over, stopped the car, and his passenger got out. The man walked across the street and to Earl's surprise stuck out his thumb again—indicating that he wanted to hitch back through the desert. So Earl called to him, "Hey! I just drove you all that way. Why are you going back?!" The hitchhiker looked at Earl with a lost expression on his face and said, "Hey, man, the karma's flowing this way now . . ."

I've often thought of that traveler as the perfect example of a life that is going nowhere. He had no purpose, no goal. He was simply wandering aimlessly and without direction. As Earl told me his story, I realized the hitchhiker was a metaphor for most of humanity.

I think Solomon was right when he said, "Where there is no vision, the people perish" (Prov. 29:18, KJV). What causes a person to develop a vision? Or to lose one that once inspired him? Or to regain one that was lost? I think sooner or later we all ask ourselves those ultimate questions whose answers determine, in the most fundamental and profound ways, the eventual outcome of our lives. What is my purpose in life? What ultimately will bring the most joy or meaning to my life? *Could the hell I've just come through have anything to do with the discovery of that purpose?* These are honest questions posed by authentic and caring people. In time though, and perhaps after much trial and error, we realize that the question "Why am I here?" isn't necessarily about us only. The answer lies beyond us.

Healing and Purpose

I've noticed that when tragedy strikes, most people respond to it by defining God in four possible ways. The first three ways always end in disillusionment and grief. The fourth way shows us how *pain* can lead to *purpose,* and that in turn heals us. Let's consider the four approaches.

1. *"God doesn't exist. If he existed, this wouldn't be happening to me."* This view presumes that a loving God would never allow suffering—even though pain and anguish are the things that mature us because they compel us to think deeper and to live humble, compassionate lives. Without anguish, we simply cannot move beyond what is shallow or mundane.
2. *"God exists but he doesn't care."* This approach was articulated by deists during the Enlightenment. It sees God as a creator who wound up the universe like a clock and left it to tick on its own. It believes that God set up some rules but he is not personally involved. He is emotionally detached from his creation and therefore lacks the very love that must define a perfect God.
3. *"God exists and he cares but he is not powerful enough to fix this mess."* I have heard these words many times from people who have suffered a devastating loss. Many years ago while visiting her mother in New York City a friend of mine was raped by two men with a knife. She had two young children and was shaken terribly by the experience. It was many months before she was able to care for her children because of her trauma. During this time her husband told me, "God couldn't prevent the rape. There is too much evil in the world."
4. *"God exists. He cares, and he is powerful enough to use our anguish in a redeeming and transforming way."* This is the only view that is practical and restorative. It sees creation as an ongoing process and guarantees that when we emerge from our painful experiences we will look back and say, "I have walked through the valley of the shadow of death and *in that valley* I received wisdom, intimacy, and compassion and these could never have been mine without the anguish I knew."

I am convinced that those who wrestle with their pain in a mature and honest way will not only survive the experience but will emerge from the trauma with a new, priority-changing outlook on life. Grief and anguish are inevitable in this world, and when it happens to us our natural reaction is to retreat into a place of safety—hoping to find a way to heal *there*. It may be important to do this during the opening stages of the grieving process because we are simply too overwhelmed to think beyond ourselves, but here are some thoughts to consider: We were designed to be givers and to live in community with others. Complete healing isn't possible apart from the purposes for which we were created. I am always amazed by testimonies I have heard from people who finally found meaning and healing after some terrible loss in the act of caring for other wounded souls. In other words, real healing isn't found in the safety of a protective cloister—it is found among other broken and vulnerable people.

The city dump outside of Managua, Nicaragua, has been called one of the "20 Horrors of the Modern World" by the Spanish magazine *Interviu*. Its name is La Chureca. Two thousand families live right in the dump—scavenging for anything of value so that they can provide for themselves. The heat, the stench, and the waterless poverty permeate the air. Nothing is clean. Nothing is healthy. The children are especially vulnerable, and girls as young as nine years old are often forced into prostitution. To many, drugs and suicide are seen as the only escape.

A small mission called Villa Esperanza houses, clothes, educates, and loves a few dozen girls from this dump. What is so incredible about the mission, though, is not just what it gives to the girls. Americans and Canadians of all ages come and donate a week or two of their time at the Villa and something joyful and transformational happens when they do. Many go to that mission feeling empty and aimless but come back energized and invigorated by a new vision for their lives. There is an archaic word that I like to use to describe what happens to people who donate their time to such places. It is the word *quickened*. It means "brought back to life."

God created us for intimacy with him and others. But that creation isn't made possible simply by putting body parts together to make a man or a woman. True intimacy requires honesty, courage, and integrity and these can only be formed in a context of pain and fear. *Creation requires trauma.* When we are comfortable, we don't look deep inside ourselves. We don't even understand our need for growth or sacrifice.

Karen Kaehr, a dear friend of mine and a clinical counselor, explained the process of growth with four simple ideas. Here they are in all their glory:

1. *God won't waste your pain.* Everything has a reason. We are loved and adored by One who uses anguish to bring us to a place of meaning and joy, but this requires faith and obedience.
2. *Faith and obedience in the midst of agony is a symphony to God's ears.* We choose him in the middle of everything that is going wrong because we know he is just. He reveals himself when everything seems chaotic and senseless and says, "*Let me redeem your anguish. Let me show you why it's here.*" When the Spirit of God begins to heal and cleanse our open wounds, he is not willing to skim the surface. He will take us as deep as our pain.
3. *Faith requires letting go of former things.* When we release our grip on everything that we once thought *should* be, we allow God to supply us with a new vision—one that is actually *meant* to be.
4. *We are not unsalvageable and neither is anyone else.* When we realize that our value is rooted in the fact that God adores us, we begin to treat others as equally precious and equally priceless and that in turn restores us.

Doing Justice

I recently returned from a one-week missions trip to the inner city of Philadelphia. I was there with a fellowship of Asian-American students from Carnegie Mellon University. We spent our days cleaning out an old building that will eventually become a women's resource center, and in the evenings we went to a street corner called "hell" and handed out drinks and sandwiches to addicts and prostitutes.

We found a world of violence and brokenness. Everyone there seemed to know that they were not where they should be and yet they were too afraid to experience anything else. The unknown—no matter how liberating—can be terrifying. As we prayed with these people, they often broke down in tears because they knew how deeply enslaved they were and they were afraid of dying before ever being free. We met a few people who were ready to take a leap of faith and place their lives into the hands of a God they hardly knew. It had become clear to them that the alternative would be death.

I don't think I'll ever forget how one of the female students I was with approached a troubled man and with a sweet, sincere voice said, "Can I pray for you?" I watched as the man just melted and the walls came down and he began pouring out his sorrow. Someone had taken an interest in him. Someone had treated him with dignity. The students I was with spoke about the experience afterwards. They came to the city with no similar experiences and no preconceived ideas. They just wanted to radiate the love of God into the lives of hurting people and they wanted to be transformed by it.

When we experience personal pain we catch glimpses of who God is and our lives are deepened by a sensitivity for others. We begin to see that God's love and justice understands the vulnerability of an orphan. It acknowledges how the first few years of human life are crucial with regard to the formation of a conscience. God's justice is painfully aware of each individual's fragile existence and it takes into account all the harmful influences that combined to produce every hopeless case in a judicial system. It analyzes a society whose moral fabric is disintegrating and it rushes to redeem. Like the Good Shepherd it leaves the protected flock to search for that one lost lamb whose life is endangered. In other words, justice is an equalizing force—a jubilee that restores one who has been disinherited to a position of dignity. It gives power to the powerless. It is the voice of the voiceless. It defends the defenseless. Believers believe these things because an All-Consuming Fire threw billions of galaxies across light years of space and then took a personal interest in each of us—despite our feebleness and our pretenses of power—and by so doing, established our pricelessness forever.

While I was in Philadelphia, I met a young man named Harry. When Harry was about six years old and living in a slum, his home caught fire. His younger brother and sister perished. His father wasn't in his life and his mother fell apart. She turned to drugs and then prostitution to support her habit. That's the atmosphere that Harry grew up in. As he grew older, he made some poor choices and found himself in prison. After several years, his experiences compelled him to begin asking some deeper questions about where he was and where he should be. All of his pain and anger brought him to a place where he wondered what God may have in store for him if he were to finally surrender his life. When God brings us to such a place through anguish and suffering, this is what he says:

> For I know the plans I have for you, . . . plans for your welfare and not for evil, to give you a future and a hope. Then you will call upon me and come and pray to me, and I will hear you. You will seek me and find me; when you seek me with all your heart.
> (Jer. 29:11–13)

Harry is now leading missions teams to the hardest streets of Philadelphia. He is adored and honored by hundreds of college students who donate their time to serve beside him, and his life is now full of meaning and hope. He is a young man who is living out the principle that God is real and caring and powerful and that if we place our lives into his loving arms, *pain will lead to purpose* and we will be transformed. This principle is so counter intuitive and paradoxical but it has been proven true over and over. Pain leads to joy when God is believed.

Let's take this a little deeper. Any conversation about the justice and compassion of God must lead eventually to Jesus. Of all the unpredictable and paradoxical things that God has done, the thing that is most contrary to human nature and therefore most baffling to us is the Incarnation. Christians believe that the Incarnation—the coming of God in human flesh was the pivotal event in human history. It stuns us the way it stunned the Greco-Roman world of the first century. Why would an almighty God present himself as the lowest of the low? Why would an almighty God divest himself of his greatness and become something seemingly insignificant? Why would an almighty God allow himself to be humiliated, tortured, and executed? The life and teachings of Jesus would make no sense to any human mind that is bent on creating God in its own image. We want power and safety. God wants something else.

As the significance of the Incarnation began to be understood by Jesus' disciples, they marveled at it. They were to others poor, powerless, and insignificant Jews in a land governed and oppressed by a formidable foreign army. Why would an omnipotent God come to *them* rather than the Emperor? Why would he choose to demonstrate his kind of power through *their* kind of powerlessness? They wondered about these things and found the Incarnation to be a gorgeous declaration of the iconoclastic brilliance of God.

In choosing those who were at the bottom of the world's social ladder, God showed that his priorities were not the world's priorities and that his methods would be different from any other power. He gravitated towards and identified with the weakest of the weak and through that weakness he made himself known. Stunned by this knowledge, Mary declared:

> "My soul magnifies the Lord,
> and my spirit rejoices in God my Savior,
> for he has regarded the low estate of his handmaiden. . . .
> He has scattered the proud in the imagination of their hearts,
> he has put down the mighty from their thrones,
> and exalted those of low degree; he has filled the hungry with good things, and the rich he has sent empty away."
>
> (Luke 1:46–53)

When Jesus began his ministry, his first public statement reinforced this declaration:

> The Spirit of the Lord is upon me, because he has anointed me to preach good news to the poor. He has sent me to proclaim release to the captives and recovering of sight to the blind, to set at liberty those who are oppressed . . .
>
> (Luke 4:18)

Paul, in his letter to the Philippians writes,

> Have this mind among yourselves, which is yours in Christ Jesus, who, though he was in the form of God, did not count equality with God a thing to be grasped, but emptied himself, taking the form of a servant, being born in the likeness of men. And being found in human form he humbled himself and became obedient unto death, even death on a cross.
>
> (Phil. 2:5–8)

Throughout biblical history, God is portrayed as One who identifies with the weak rather than the powerful. But the Philippians passage takes it one step further. The phrase *emptied himself* is translated from the Greek word *kenosis,* which literally means "divested himself." One cannot divest oneself of anything unless one possesses it in the first place. The Bible teaches that Christ was divine and yet he valued something more than the power of the divine. He valued us. He demonstrated this by becoming a servant and suffering for our sake. This portrayal is as contrary to human nature as it is *deep*. We seek security and power, God seeks justice and mercy. Power indulges itself. Love empties itself. Every person who wishes to make a name for himself seizes power and wields it, but when God divested himself of power, he became the most prominent person in human history. Why did he do it? What was he trying to tell us? *One thing is certain, our healing and purpose in life, must have something to do with the character and priorities of the One who made us.*

In scripture, whenever someone was called by God that call was accompanied by a commission to act in the world.[18] Conversion isn't simply about emotional happiness and personal peace of mind. It is taking up a cross and following Christ. The question 'Why am I here?' can't really be answered without a clear understanding of *who God is* and how he uses the dynamic of pain to complete his creation in us. Replacing God with religion will only leave us empty. Something else must take place *deep within us* before life will have any significance or meaning. Becoming more and more like Christ means surrendering all those things that we cling to for safety. There is no victory apart from surrender. There is no power apart from divestment. There is no healing love apart from anguish and intimacy.

Consider the first ten verses of Isaiah 58:

> [1] "Shout it aloud, do not hold back.
>   Raise your voice like a trumpet.
> Declare to my people their rebellion
>   and to the descendants of Jacob their sins.
> [2] For day after day they seek me out;
>   they seem eager to know my ways,
> as if they were a nation that does what is right
>   and has not forsaken the commands of its God.
> They ask me for just decisions
>   and seem eager for God to come near them.
> [3] 'Why have we fasted,' they say,
>   'and you have not seen it?
> Why have we humbled ourselves,
>   and you have not noticed?'
>
> "Yet on the day of your fasting, you do as you please
>   and exploit all your workers.

⁴ Your fasting ends in quarreling and strife,
   and in striking each other with wicked fists.
You cannot fast as you do today
   and expect your voice to be heard on high.
⁵ Is this the kind of fast I have chosen,
   only a day for people to humble themselves?
Is it only for bowing one's head like a reed
   and for lying in sackcloth and ashes?
Is that what you call a fast,
   a day acceptable to the LORD?

⁶ "Is not this the kind of fasting I have chosen:
to loose the chains of injustice
   and untie the cords of the yoke,
to set the oppressed free
   and break every yoke?
⁷ Is it not to share your food with the hungry
   and to provide the poor wanderer with shelter—
when you see the naked, to clothe them,
   and not to turn away from your own flesh and blood?
⁸ Then your light will break forth like the dawn,
   and your healing will quickly appear;
then your righteousness[a] will go before you,
   and the glory of the LORD will be your rear guard.
⁹ Then you will call, and the LORD will answer;
   you will cry for help, and he will say: Here am I.

"If you do away with the yoke of oppression,
with the pointing finger and malicious talk,
¹⁰ and if you spend yourselves in behalf of the hungry
   and satisfy the needs of the oppressed,
then your light will rise in the darkness,
   and your night will become like the noonday. (NIV)

There is a pair of spiritual bookends in these ten verses. The passage begins with religious people asking, "Where are you, God?" It ends with God saying, "I've been here all along but I don't reside in rituals. I make myself known when the poor and the weak are loved." When we ask, "Why am I here?" the answer must include the word *love*. This passage from Isaiah exposes the classic confrontation between religion and relationship. We weren't created for religion. We were created for intimacy, and the glory of that intimacy with God is that it gives rise to a self-sacrificing love for vulnerable people and that in turn *restores our souls*.

Loving Mercy

Thirty-eight years ago on a hot summer's evening, I was visiting the home of my high school girlfriend. She lived not too far from the Long Island Sound and her family had spent the day at the beach. Her father was a solid man with greying hair and a lovable disposition. He had been waterskiing all day long and was now looking for some relaxation, so he suggested a Walt Disney movie. We all agreed and eagerly climbed into his car to begin the fifteen mile drive to the theater.

We never made it. Halfway to the theater, Mr. Sutherland suddenly pulled over to the side of the road and said, "I don't think it's prudent for us to go any further." The rest of us just looked at each other and wondered what was wrong. A second later, his body shook and then slumped over onto the steering wheel. We didn't know it at the time but he was in the middle of a heart attack. All we knew was that he needed attention immediately, so his wife jumped out of the car and ran around to the driver's side. She pushed her husband into the passenger seat and began to drive. The hospital was back where we had come from. The speed limit on that road was perhaps 45 mph, but within minutes we were zipping along at 80. The story ended happily and Mr. Sutherland recovered nicely, but consider what could have happened if our car had been stopped by a police officer. . .

Matters of law and faith can be approached in two very different ways. Some people choose a rigid, legalistic approach; others are more understanding and gracious. If a legalistic police officer had stopped our car that day in 1972, his only question would be whether the driver was speeding. The speed limit was clearly marked and the violation of the law was obvious. If the driver tried to explain her situation, the officer might reply, "Ma'am, I don't make the rules, I only enforce them. If you have a problem with the speed limits, you can talk with the judge, you can call the select board, you can write to your legislator. My job is to hand out tickets. Have a nice day."

A more compassionate response would be one that understands that justice doesn't exist in a vacuum. Justice has to do with real people, real problems, and real pain. In that sense, it is contextual. Such a view requires a deeper level of inquiry. It isn't merely concerned with the letter of the law but with the spirit of the law as well. A compassionate approach may ask what the lawgiver intended by the law and whether the context should affect how the law is applied. In this case, a speed limit is intended to save lives. Rushing a gravely ill person to the hospital is also an attempt to save a life. The letter of the law may be violated, but the spirit of the law was identical to the spirit of the speeding driver. The officer who acknowledges this would tell the woman to follow his cruiser, and together they would *speed* to the hospital. Legalism provides no room for such mercy.

Jesus was confronted by legalistic people when he violated the letter of the law by healing on the Sabbath. His response was, "What would you do if your ox fell in a ditch on the Sabbath?" (Luke 14:5, author's paraphrase). Confronted again, he declared, "The Sabbath was made for man, not man for the Sabbath" (Mark 2:27, NIV). Jesus taught that merely keeping the letter of the law is not how to please God, because *a perfect law can only be applied perfectly in a perfect world.* Living in an imperfect world means being placed in positions where the moral choices we face are not always black and white. Very often we are asked to choose between the greater of two goods or the lesser of two evils. No one likes such choices but they are part of life.

Sometimes we embrace legalism because we want to pretend that moral ambiguities simply don't exist. But we live in a world where people have heart attacks on highways, oxen fall into ditches on the Sabbath, and presidents have to decide whether to drop an atomic weapon on 100,000 civilians or lose a million soldiers by ending a war conventionally.

Sometimes we face choices that seem impossible, even obscene. No matter what we do, someone is going to be hurt, or some valid principle is going to be violated. I suppose it's all part of living in a messed-up world, but I also believe that God understands our predicament. By choosing to engage us, he has faced such choices himself. The crucifixion of Christ was one such choice. "It is better... that one man die for the people than that the whole nation perish" (John 11:50, NIV). When God chose to "pitch his tent among us," he pitched it on a slippery slope. By engaging humanity, he entered into a painful world with complex moral dilemmas. His love for humanity prevented him from retreating to a safer place. The Incarnation was the willingness of God to deal directly with a fallen world, even if it meant having to choose between the lesser of two evils. He allowed for the torture and execution of an innocent man to accomplish the redemption of us all. He didn't elevate dead orthodoxies over divine compassion. He loved us too much for that.

There are many people who are so weighed down by guilt that they can't draw close to God. They have been unable to forgive themselves after making difficult choices. They did their best to minimize damage but damage was done anyway. They didn't have the luxury of a choice between good and evil. Maybe they chose to be divorced from an alcoholic spouse. Maybe they left an abusive relationship and felt that they were betraying a loved one. God understands these dilemmas. He understands the heartache. He understands what it's like to make such a choice and to be demonized by pharisees who love laws more than God. Sometimes, dear reader, we need to just go to him with humility and sorrow and receive his grace.

Walking Humbly

I remember happy times. I remember a loving wife and adoring children. I remember close friends deciding to have several children because they had seen my wife and I succeeding at raising ours. I remember camping with my boys and snuggling at bedtime with my girls. I remember changing diapers and nursing wounds, music lessons and soccer games, school plays and homework preparations—and all those other activities that parents do to love their children.

I remember struggling financially yet never being without the things we needed. I remember making furniture for my family and toys for my kids. I remember a kindly old man in the antiques business who came to my house one day when my young family and I needed to raise some cash. We showed him an antique cupboard we had refinished and asked if he would buy it. He said, "Why do you want to sell it? It's beautiful." I replied, "We's jus' po' folk. We need the dollars." He shook his head and said, "You're not poor. You just don't have any money." I remember being dazzled by that wisdom. I remember realizing then that I have never been poor. I have always felt wealthy and blessed even when I was unemployed and desperate. I remember when my young family and I went from homelessness to owning a small, successful business—all within six months and all by the grace of God. I remember a continual succession of God's blessings that convinced me in my naivete that I must certainly be doing something right.

When Justin was a little boy, I would tuck him in bed at night and he'd say, "Daddy, 'pend a little time with me?" We would make forts out of refrigerator boxes. We played laser tag, threw water balloons, and planned scavenger hunts. I remember tossing Lego grenades into my two sons' bedroom and watching them run into the hallway as fast as they could before the imaginary explosion could give me the chance to say, "I won! I won!" I remember losing an arm wrestle with my son for the first time and seeing Justin's glee over his accomplishment. Once, I got him in a full nelson as we wrestled on the living room floor, knowing that I would probably never beat him in anything again because he had become so big and strong.

I remember my son Nathaniel and my daughter Lisa preparing a candlelit multi-course dinner in front of the living room fireplace for their mom and me on our anniversary.

I remember helping to plan Emily's eighth grade trip to Canada. The parents and their children met in the middle school library. All the adults were on one side of the room and all the young teenagers were on the other side—each one unwilling to be seen with their parents. But my daughter sat beside me on a tabletop with her arms around me and her head on my shoulder as if she didn't care at all what anyone thought of her. I recall feeling so loved and so proud.

Before that school year came to an end, my world collapsed. Three years earlier, my wife had taken a job at a crisis counseling center. It was filled with unhealthy, addictive personalities. She came home one day and said, "There's a guy at work who's been coming on to me with inappropriate terms of affection." He was an alcoholic who had failed in everything he tried and he was now trying his hand at counseling. He didn't raise his children. He bounced from one sick relationship to another. My wife had handled these situations well previously but this time would be different.

A few days before Emily's eighth-grade graduation, my wife took me into a hallway where all of our children's photographs were hanging on the wall. She pointed to the smiling faces and said, "We've had twenty-five years together and raised four happy children, but I don't love you anymore and I want a divorce." A few days later, I discovered an e-mail in the family computer. It was addressed to "dear sweetie." An affair had destroyed my marriage. On the day she left, my wife of twenty-five years put her hand on my shoulder and said, "You were a good man."

It would be easy on my ego if I just ended this story here, but what followed next for me was a long, painful period of discovery where I was forced to look deep inside myself and see something extraordinarily upsetting. The betrayal had left me a very angry person.

FINDING OUR PLACE ON THE SLIPPERY SLOPE (WHY AM I HERE?) | 73

I'm told that adultery affects fifty percent of all marriages in America, and I suppose my experience is far from unique. But for me, as brutal as adultery is it was not the most painful thing. The hardest part was being blamed for my wife's failure. When that happened, I went ballistic. I wanted to skewer any person who wagged his head at me.

I have a dear friend in California who was married for thirty-five years to an alcoholic and had suffered through her spouse's numerous affairs. When her marriage finally ended, her brother-in-law approached her one day and said, "You must have been awfully cold in the bedroom for my brother to have had all those affairs." There was an automatic assumption that the faithful spouse was at fault. Her husband's alcoholism and all the childhood pain behind it was never even considered. Words like that have a way of turning hurt into rage.

I've noticed that not all human beings are angered by the same things. I know a person with a serious anxiety disorder. She is angered by fear. Another person may have no ability to show remorse for her mistakes and doesn't know what to do with her failures. She is angered by guilt.

I am not angered by fear or guilt. I am angered by powerlessness. I remember being beat up by a classmate when I was about twelve years old. A circle of kids formed around me and I was picked up over the bully's head and spun around and around in a dizzying dance of humiliating scorn until I was thrown to the ground as everyone laughed. That day, a hatred of powerlessness became etched into my personality. It is so easy for me to feel anger when things begin to spin out of control.

When I practiced law, nearly all of my clients were victims of abuse. Most were women. For some reason, they wanted to stay with men who demeaned them and abandoned them emotionally and financially. These men wanted sex but not responsibility. They were constantly being compelled by the courts to pay child support. I would take an interest in my clients' children and fill their refrigerators with food and they would wonder why their husbands couldn't do the same. But my wife traded me in for an alcoholic even while acknowledging that I had been a good husband. I was powerless to make sense of it. I felt as though twenty-five years of goodness had suddenly been negated and my inability to do anything about it was consuming me.

Letting Go

It took me a while to realize that it was futile to base my healing on the hope that someone someday would say, "I'm sorry." Some people aren't capable of that and I knew that if I didn't overcome my anger, it would affect all of my other relationships. I had reached the point where I wasn't going to put up with anything from anybody, and if my teenagers began to give me some attitude, I would detonate a thermo-emotional device over their psyche. I needed help.

Something told me that I had to take the focus off of me. Being hurt is an event. It doesn't have to be a lifelong trauma. I realized that it was time to look at my life through a wide-angle lens. The focus had to be on something bigger than me. Others meant this pain for evil but God meant it for good. I began asking myself, "What do you see? God? Or the tempest?" I finally realized that adultery can be a gift. The marriage and its aftermath had left me hungering for something that only God could give.

But acknowledging these things isn't the same as healing. I needed to take some steps of faith. The first step was to allow God to place me in his care and remove me from those who justified their behavior by distorting my character. Those comments simply reopen old wounds. The second step involved caring for wholesome people who needed help. By serving someone who was capable of showing gratitude and grace, I actually found myself growing stronger.

It wasn't easy realizing what an angry person I had become. I had always pictured myself as a compassionate and caring man, but during this ordeal I saw the violence in my soul. I knew I had no power to fix it. I only had the power to screw things up more. I have no idea what would have become of me without an understanding of the power of God to heal and the grace that he offers. My powerlessness brought me to my knees before that Consuming Fire, and then once again a wormhole in the cosmos appeared.

The Empowering Paradox

Now I'm glad—not that you were upset, but that you were jarred into turning things around. You let the distress bring you to God, not drive you from him. The result was all gain, no loss. Distress that drives us to God does that. It turns us around. It gets us back in the way of salvation. We never regret that kind of pain. But those who let distress drive them away from God are full of regrets, end up on a deathbed of regrets.

(2 Cor. 7:8–10, The Message)

Three times I besought the Lord about this, that it should leave me; but he said to me, "My grace is sufficient for you, for my power is made perfect in weakness." I will all the more gladly boast of my weaknesses, that the power of Christ may rest upon me. For the sake of Christ, then, I am content with weaknesses, insults, hardships, persecutions, and calamities; for when I am weak, then I am strong.

(2 Cor. 12:8–10)

The journey towards healing seems so counterintuitive. God says that my power produces nothing of eternal significance, but my weakness enables him to work profoundly and powerfully through me. When we ask ourselves Why am I here?, the answer must contain something of this paradox. We are here to do justice and to love mercy, but there is one more thing that makes those things possible. It is the humble act of acknowledging our inadequacies. With that humility we are changed from the inside out and the power of *that* process can transform the world.

I'm sure that every person reading this can relate to the experience of betrayal. It is nothing unusual, but it is disheartening because the word *betrayal* suggests some prior intimacy. We don't feel betrayed by enemies. We feel betrayed by those we once trusted. Billy Graham once was called "the worst thing that ever happened to American Evangelicalism." This charge was leveled against him not by a secular press but by a well known fundamentalist. When I heard the charge, I shook my head in disbelief. If a fundamentalist can view Billy Graham as "the worst thing," is it any wonder that the Messiah was crucified?

Graham expected rejection from skeptics. It didn't bother him. But when someone is vilified by a person in his own family, it wounds the soul like nothing else can. Billy Graham faced that woundedness with honor and grace. He didn't return evil for evil. He trusted in the power and plan of God so that when the tempest raged, he was secure. I needed to be shown that. I needed to be shown that my security and my value could only be found in something permanent and eternal and that finding my place on this slippery slope meant understanding the depths of my weaknesses and the sufficiency of God's grace.

6

Till My Trophies at Last I Lay Down (Where Am I Going?)

My dad was a fine artist in New York. He painted still lifes, landscapes, and portraits of wealthy people. He also had a strong belief in the love of God and taught his children to integrate faith and vocation and to be a good steward of whatever gifts we had. It was not uncommon for my siblings and me to hear my dad refer to the Parable of the Good Steward (Matt. 25:14–30) as we sat around the dinner table during our formative years. That parable meant a lot to him. It's a story about men who were given various amounts of wealth and told to invest them wisely while their master was away. One steward did very well with his investments, another did reasonably well, but another was afraid of losing everything, so he hid his money and made no attempt to honor his master's wishes. When the master returned, each was rewarded for his stewardship, while the one who acted out of fear, received no reward but, in fact, got a good scolding.

My dad impressed on us the importance of discovering our gifts and giving our best effort to honor God with them. It was a pretty weighty thing. At times, there seemed to be no room for screwing up. The problem with parables is that they do a great job illustrating one part of a truth without necessarily giving the whole picture. For instance, what happens when we fail? Is there forgiveness? Do we get another chance? If those questions aren't answered in a compassionate way, we could develop an unhealthy way of seeing everything.

It was impressed on me early that I needed to perform well. I still remember Dad quoting the words *pressed down, shaken together, running over* (Luke 6:38). That was the measure that I was to give. It wasn't an oppressive thing—at least it wasn't intended that way because my dad, being a lifelong Lutheran, had spent many years marinating in a culture that emphasized grace over works. But throughout my formative years I was encouraged to live a productive life so that one day I would be able to hear God say, "Well done, good and faithful servant" (Matt. 25:23).

Performance and Grace

Taken in isolation, that teaching can mess up a person. Over time, I felt that I had to set higher and higher goals and after reaching each successive goal, I would feel as though it wasn't enough. It would never be enough. There was always something greater to do. After a while, but when I was still a young man, I realized that I could never succeed because the standard was so impossibly high.

In 1983, I completed a master's degree and was appointed to a research fellowship at Yale University. I went to visit my dad and was sitting in his studio as he painted my portrait. He knew my vocational goals and he encouraged me to aim higher and higher and not be content to influence hundreds of people but to try instead to alter the course of history and change the lives of millions of people. My dad was a good man. He meant well. I respected him for encouraging me. But as I felt the huge burden to change the lives of so many, I finally said, "Dad, who am I going to perform for when you're gone?"

My dad seemed stunned by the question. He had no idea that I had absorbed the teaching the way I had. Suddenly, stewardship and grace were at odds with each other. At some point we come to realize that trying to find our sense of worth in life by producing more and more stuff—even if it's *good* stuff—doesn't satisfy us and in fact leaves us disillusioned, empty, and feeling like failures.

A short while later, Dad was diagnosed with cancer. I called his physician and asked if the condition was terminal. The doctor answered curtly, "Mr. Kautz, *life* is terminal." My dad died one day before my thirty-fifth birthday. He had sent me a card in the mail that I received after his death. It was like a note from the grave. In the card, Dad affirmed me. He called me a "beloved son." He spoke of my young family and business and the joy of having my whole life ahead of me. He let me know that I had pleased him.

I think I would have cried no matter what he said because, after all, he was gone and these were his final remarks to me. But the fact that I was accepted as I was, with flaws and blemishes and without having altered the course of human history, caused my tears to flow like an open spigot. He had been such a powerful force in my life and I had sometimes wondered whether I would ever be able to wow him the way he seemed to want. But here he was . . . satisfied. It was over. The impossible quest for value ended with a few thoughtful words. All those years of feeling as though I needed to measure up to an impossible standard suddenly had been replaced with something called *grace*.

This point was driven further home to me at my dad's funeral. I remember approaching his casket and seeing the paint brushes that my brother had placed in his hands. There is something surreal about looking directly at someone and at the same time not seeing him at all. I was just looking at a shell. He was no longer there. Those were *his* facial features. Those were *his* hands I held. But they were cold and what little remained would soon be gone—nothing more than bone, dust, and hair, all matted together in some awful mess. It spoke to me not really of the *finality* of life because I don't believe in its finality, but of the *vulnerability* of all flesh. The fact that someone who was once so powerful should also be so frail as to die argues for grace. It argues for each one of us to wonder in amazement how vulnerable we all are and how our relationships with the living must be defined by tenderness and mercy.

The longer I live, the more I see how starved for grace we all are. Every broken heart, every damaged soul, every human institution, every social structure, every loser, every winner, and every disillusioned ex-idealist seems to be crying out for mercy. The cry is mostly inaudible. After all, to cry out loud is to expose oneself. So most choose silence—*as if an emaciated body could ever conceal its hunger*. We don't need to *hear* the cry of others. It's just there and obvious. We all fail and we all yearn to be valued despite our failures. But from our earliest years, we are beaten down with gracelessness.

One day when I was in high school, I was required to play football in an intramural game. When the game began, the opposing team kicked the ball down the field and I watched as it slowly fell from the sky into my waiting arms. It had been sent high into the air and the ball seemed to take forever to reach me. During its descent, my opponents were rushing down the field towards me and I was their reluctant target. I'm not a jock. I don't have the agility or the coordination of an athlete. I'm sure someone else would have performed much better than me that day. I just remember an awful sense of doom as each eternal second of that ball's descent meant the opposing team would rush closer and closer to me.

By the time I finally caught that ball, I could take only a few steps before I was tackled. One of my teammates was not pleased with me. "You have sh_t for brains!" he screamed. For the rest of the game, and the rest of that week, he took it upon himself to hurl obscenities at me. He didn't grow tired of it until he found another person to malign and another way to validate himself. It would be easy to assume that the person in this story who was being cursed at was the one in need of grace. Failing to dodge some football players was embarrassing but I wasn't as upset as my irate teammate. I was the kind of kid who would have just shrugged and said, "Dude! It's *not* the NFL. Cut me some slack!" The guy who was screaming obscenities at me may have been more in need of grace than I was at the time. One has to be wounded to behave that way. Mine was merely an athletic failure. His revealed a deeper despair.

Later that same week, I was sitting in a lecture hall waiting for a guest speaker along with 150 of my classmates. It was 1971 and the Vietnam War was still polarizing the nation. Signs of the counterculture were everywhere on campus and the guest speaker would be addressing some current issue. But he never showed up and the crowd of students began to get restless. Suddenly someone remembering that "Kautz has sh_t for brains" decided to put me on the spot—suggesting that I address the class instead of the tardy lecturer. I had recently come to faith and people knew it and wanted me to explain myself. Like a football descending into my arms, all of my classmates began chanting, "Kautz! Kautz! Kautz!"

I thought, *What the heck*. For some reason, that football seemed to fall into my arms without even a moment's wait and strangely, I felt like I had been called to receive it. I walked down the sloping floor to the well of the lecture hall and looked up at 150 grinning classmates who fully expected me to entertain them with nonsense.

I remember that for the next half hour as I shared my faith, words began flowing out of me like it was the most natural thing in the world. I remember the grins disappearing and being replaced by a collection of thoughtful countenances. That surprised me because in my high school cruel was cool. Most of all, I remember the pensive silence of my classmates. It was the first time I had ever addressed a group. I tried to speak from the heart and to touch that wounded emptiness that must exist in everyone because we all live in a world where footballs fall into unprepared arms and thousands of our insecure peers are desperate to console themselves with their hopeless, jeering obscenities.

Later that week, people approached me and kindly said that they would never ridicule me again. Some came to faith by that experience, others didn't, but each comment I received seemed to acknowledge that there was something *mysteriously redemptive about identifying the hollow, aching hunger in each of our souls.*

The act of identifying that hunger can sometimes be unpleasant. What person wants to be reminded of pain? Who wants to look for cancer in a stool sample? There is nothing appealing about blood and excrement. But there can be no healing without a diagnosis. For many, when the hunger is identified, the response is instant indignation. It is as if a diagnosis of lymphoma has just been rendered and the first step in the grieving process is denial followed by rage. It's valid to ask that we be protected from *evil*. It is *not* valid to ask that we be protected from *truth*. When our response is "Shoot the messenger," "Punish the person who identifies the problem," or "Hate the doctor," it speaks not only of woundedness but of arrogance as well. There is neither maturity nor redemption in such emotions. There is instead, a pathology of fear evidenced by distrust, exile, isolation, lost communion, resentment, truth loathing, and an inability to know what to do with one's inadequacies or one's weakness. It is terrified of transparency. It seeks the pretense of safety but not the true significance or security of grace because *that grace* begs to be preceded by a broken and contrite heart. Apart from such a heart, there can be neither emotional healing or scholastic integrity.

For others, the identification of their hunger is greeted with hope and even joy. I once read of a woman who had battled depression for years and never knew she was depressed. When a doctor diagnosed her, she said, "Finally, my enemy has a name!" For her, it was liberating just to know that the problem could be identified and understood. She was ready for the next step.

Jesus said, "You will know the truth, and the truth will make you free" (John 8:32). It is the Spirit of God—that All-Consuming Fire—that gives voice to the deepest groans and most profound yearnings of the human heart and suggests to us that those yearnings can only be satisfied by our Maker.

But the idea that this satisfaction can be found in the externals of religion is perhaps the most devious of deceptions. That deception says, "Come to God. He can heal you," and then it immediately replaces the Person of God with mere precepts and very often, graceless dogma. It is, in the end, a call to idolatry. It draws its strength from guilt rather than a hunger for intimacy. It says "performance is everything"—making grace irrelevant.

When I practiced law, one of my first clients was a young Christian woman who had been abused by her husband. I will call her Gail. Married in her early twenties, everything seemed fine at first. But as the pressures of life began to mount, Gail's husband suddenly exhibited the first signs of mental illness. He was initially diagnosed with bipolar disorder but his condition later deteriorated into some form of psychosis. He became paranoid and would often run into the closet when an airplane flew overhead. He was convinced the CIA was spying on him. At one point he chased his little children with an ax. Gail took her kids and hid somewhere safe. She was in a difficult position economically and I asked her minister if some help could be offered.

Later that week, in a meeting with the elders of the church, the pastor commented that Gail had married a damaged man and that this indicated something lacking in her. That comment was made over fourteen years ago and I still marvel at it. Sometimes a person's mind can understand the *theory* of grace and yet never actually know how to *live* grace because he's never been broken. What is in the heart, I suppose, eventually comes out. Two things need to be observed here. The first is obvious: *There is something lacking in all of us* and that is precisely why grace is offered. The second is that there was no initial evidence of mental illness when Gail's marriage took place so why would anyone want to fault a woman when her spouse got sick?

The same church is blessed with a member who is a retired psychiatrist. The psychiatrist has had decades of experience diagnosing various illnesses and yet was surprised when a bipolar disorder showed up in someone he knew very well for years. If a trained psychiatrist can be surprised by the onset of such an illness, why would a pastor hold a twenty-five-year-old woman with no psychiatric training to a higher standard of discernment? There could be any number of reasons for such graceless behavior, but what I would like to note is Gail's response. Gail was probably suffering some form of post-traumatic stress. Her life and her children's lives had been threatened and she was clearly on edge. She was also filled with shame because she knew how people can talk. She knew how a church can preach grace perfectly and offer something else. Her response was so human: *"I just want to go where no one knows me."* A few years later, the leadership of the same church wondered whether a wrong message would be sent if a woman who had been divorced was permitted to sing a solo in church. *Is there fundamentally any difference between the believer who questions whether a divorced person should sing in church and an unbeliever who tells his teammate that he has sh_t for brains?* Dude! This isn't the NFL. It is the church of a gracious God who once declared, "Go and learn what this means, 'I desire mercy, and not religious rituals.'" (author's paraphrase, Matt. 9:13).

Justin liked to write. He had been a journalism major in college. One of the topics that he found most compelling was exile. He looked around his world and saw millions of hurting souls—each one yearning for safety and hungering for something that eludes them even in churches that preach the grace of God. He noticed that when we are hurt, we naturally retreat into a place that seems protective but really isn't. When that happens we are tempted to say, *"I will never be safe until I'm alone"* or *"I just want to go where nobody knows me."* Such words are uttered whenever we feel that there is no reasonable expectation of grace. Sometimes a church can cause a person to retreat into solitude because the "grace" it preaches is no grace at all. Abraham Heschel wrote this in his book *The Insecurity of Freedom:*

> The righteous lives by his faith, not by his creed. And faith is not an allegiance to a verbal formulation; on the contrary, it involves profound awareness of the inadequacy of words, concepts, deeds. Unless we realize that dogmas are tentative rather than final, that they are accommodations rather than definitions, intimations rather than descriptions; unless we learn how to share the moment and the insight to which they are trying to testify, we stand guilty of literal-mindedness, of pretending to know what cannot be put into words; we are guilty of intellectual idolatry.[19]

TILL MY TROPHIES AT LAST I LAY DOWN (WHERE AM I GOING?) | 85

Graceless religion is no less smug, and perhaps more so, than the intellectual narcissism of the secular Enlightenment. It petrifies dogmas and hardens hearts so that anyone who yearns for intimacy with a deep, awesome, ineffable, mysterious, forgiving God would be repulsed by its frozen haughtiness. Why would anyone want a whitewashed tomb instead of *life* itself? Let's hear again from Abraham Heschel:

> More frustrating than the fact that evil is real, mighty, and tempting is the fact that it thrives so well in the disguise of the good, and that it can draw its nutriment from the life of the holy. In this world, it seems, the holy and the unholy do not exist apart but are mixed, interrelated, and confounded.[20]

I once knew a young woman who had rebelled against her father. The rebellion was total and the relationship completely broken. For several years there had been no communication. After a while, there was a reconciliation of sorts but it was an awkward reunion. There were apologies but something was missing. A distance was still unconquered. The woman told me that from the time of her reconciliation to the time of her father's death, she never felt that she could ever call him Daddy again. She was too ashamed for intimacy. She longed to return to the way things had once been—when she would sit on his lap or help him fix a lawn mower.

If I was the daddy of such a girl, I would want to sandwich her face between my hands. I would want her to know that in life or in death I adored her still. I would want us to laugh at our failures and our foolishness and just cradle each other in our arms knowing that nothing could ever separate us as long as our hearts were contrite and God's grace was known. I would let her know that she was precious and priceless and that I would give my life for her. I wouldn't give her a stone instead of bread. I wouldn't give her religion instead of relationship. I wouldn't give her dogmas instead of intimacy. I wouldn't give her death instead of life. I would just say, "Come home, honey. I don't care about the past. I only care about you." Isn't this what God longs to say to us?

Grace and Peace

A few months after I came to faith, my father was given a commission to do several paintings from the life of Christ. I was still in high school at the time and was asked to help him with one of the paintings. I naively agreed without making any inquiries, and a few days later my dad informed me that he needed to do an anatomical study of a crucified body. The next thing I knew I was standing in my underwear while two of my buddies were throwing ropes over a large horizontal beam that ran across the cathedral ceiling of my father's studio. The ropes were tied to my wrists and while Dad assured me that "this will only take a few minutes," my friends slowly tugged on the ropes until I was lifted up to the beam, which was about ten feet off the ground.

As soon as my feet left the floor I felt unimaginable pain. It was all concentrated on my armpits and chest and it was like nothing I had ever felt before. My dad had several tripods with cameras set up around my body so that he could take photographs from different angles. After a few excruciating minutes, I was mercifully lowered to the ground while Dad readjusted the tripods. Once that was done, my friends raised me to the beam again and the photographing resumed. This went on for about a half hour and when the episode was over, I had a new understanding of the love of God. I hadn't been scourged the night before—nor had I been beaten beyond human semblance. But for a half hour I caught a small glimpse of true agony.

Two weeks later, my armpits still ached. I can't even imagine what it would have been like to hang there for six hours. I began to think about the nature of divine love. In its purest form, love is so self-sacrificing that we have a hard time wrapping our minds around it. The idea of a love that is willing to endure unbearable evil for the sake of another person is almost inconceivable, but for *God* to endure such evil for the sake of those who don't even know him or who are hurling insults at him boggles our minds.

The Romans were not the first to crucify their opponents. Other civilizations used stakes and crossbeams to publicly humiliate their enemies, but the Romans perfected the technique by allowing the centurions in charge of each execution to indulge their own sadistic pleasures as each case warranted. Consequently, there was no prescribed method. Some unfortunates were executed on a simple vertical stake; others were crucified on a T-shaped cross. After the Romans destroyed Jerusalem in 70 AD, they crucified thousands of Jews on whatever lumber they could find. Many were crucified on the siege works that had been built against the city walls. Some criminals would be crucified at the place of their crime—beside a city street where all could witness the justice of Rome and be terrified into submission.

Crucifixion was considered the worst of deaths. The condemned person would be stripped naked and thoroughly humiliated. It was also very unusual for a crucified body to be buried. Most were left to rot on the cross. One historian recorded that a certain Roman was eating a meal when a dog entered his house with a decaying human foot that had fallen from an executed body. The reason that the Greco-Roman mind of the first century found it so hard to embrace Christianity was that it couldn't fathom a God who was so defined by love that he would actually submit to such a detestable and shameful death in order to redeem the world he loved.

But what was inconceivable and scandalous was also profoundly and strangely beautiful. When we consider that this divine love was exhibited because we were seen as precious and priceless despite our failings, it causes us to fall to our knees with wonder and awe and realize the utter foolishness of clinging to our own mediocre accomplishments rather than the grace of God.

> *So I'll cherish the old rugged cross,*
> *Till my trophies at last I lay down;*
> *I will cling to the old rugged cross,*
> *And exchange it some day for a crown.*[21]

But the Cross doesn't just speak of a redeemed humanity. Something else besides humanity was rescued at Golgotha. It was *everything*. It was *history* itself. It was all the events we have ever witnessed. The *event* of the crucifixion, as shameful and grotesque as it was, was transformed into a thing of beauty and with it, *every injustice and every heartache we have ever experienced.* A new understanding of history has been given to us. What was meant by some to impose a nauseating cruelty upon an innocent person was meant by God to do something entirely different. Joseph's words to his brothers return to us again and again: "You meant it for evil but God meant it for good." The biblical view of history is one that looks beyond evil intent and humiliating or heartbreaking events. It is a view that proclaims the sovereign grace of God over all powers and all events.

> This Jesus, delivered up according to the definite plan and foreknowledge of God, you crucified and killed by the hands of lawless men. But God raised him up . . .
>
> (Acts 2:23–24)

The above passage speaks about two intentions: the intentions of men and the intentions of God. Both are real. Neither can be denied. The two intentions have entirely different goals but only the Lover of our souls is in control of all things. The movement of God in human history is one that asks us to remove the telephoto lens from our eyes and replace it with a wide-angle perspective. It encourages us to focus on the presence of a beautiful Savior and watch as he transforms even the ugliest and most brutal events into something redemptive. A tumor, a betrayal, a cross become strangely beautiful. Like Peter, we are asked to turn our eyes towards Jesus—not towards the waves and the tempest.

It is the movement of God in our lives that calls us to see his Spirit hovering over the face of our deepest void and over all of our unfulfilled yearnings. It transforms our vision so that every disappointment, every injustice, every grief finds its meaning and its healing in the sovereign grace of God. *The intimacy you were created for is the purpose of your grief.* God rules even over anguish and evil—even over those seemingly coincidental twists of fate that take the lives of loved ones from us.

Let the avalanches come. God governs with a mystery and a splendor we can only wait to grasp. Because he is loving and sovereign, we have reason to trust. That's what faith is . . . it is knowing in the darkness that a loving God has a plan that's better than any we could ever imagine. A sovereign God adores us, and for this reason the ending of our stories will be beautiful.

7
Waking the Vision of Sleeping Dust

Grief is a strange thing. It seems to build up and build up, and then one day it all gushes out and you allow yourself the luxury of being a basket case for a day or two. Then, after the catharsis, you can function for a while as the grief begins building again. When my son died, this process repeated itself in me over and over. During my better days, after I had let it all out, I began preparing for the memorial service that had been postponed nearly two months. I decided to give the eulogy for Justin because I sensed he would have wanted me to. I tackled the job as if it were the most important thing I would ever do.

Death is always shocking, but when it comes so swiftly to a young person its horror is all the more intense. My son had had what everyone wanted. He was young and intelligent, athletic and gifted, and so full of life. I knew that this tragedy would cause some to question the love of God and the meaning of life and death. I wanted to speak to that issue and the underlying cynicism that often accompanies disappointment and loss. I wanted to comfort those who might be questioning the wisdom of God or their own purpose in life. I felt that Justin would have wanted to do that, too. He would have wanted to comfort and encourage people to go deeper because that was who he was.

When I spoke at the memorial service, I had no notes. Everything I said was from the heart. I later transcribed the audio recording into a written text for this chapter. Justin and I both enjoyed the creative process and thinking outside the box. What made him special was the depth of his conversations, the origin of his values, and the nature of our shared faith. So on the day of his memorial service, with hundreds of people watching, I stood to offer the following remarks—unsure if I could even make it past the first few thoughts, but certain that I wanted to capture those things that we once had together and to give voice to his passion for the restorative and redemptive power of God in the lives of ordinary people. . .

I would like to tell you about the last time that I saw Justin and a conversation that we had. He had been working on a collection of short stories on the topic of exile and in particular that kind of exile that we impose on ourselves when we've been hurt and we make a conscious decision to choose self-protection over relational intimacy. So we talked about this and also about integrity and courage and what it means to not just stand up for what's right—regardless of the consequences—but also to look deep inside ourselves to see what kind of gunk might lay there. We acknowledged that this kind of courage is probably the hardest kind to practice. We talked about how difficult it is for someone who's been crushed or wounded or damaged in some way to engage in any self-examination, because it's almost unbearable to look within when we aren't sure about our own value. And so our conversation led to the topic of human value, what determines it, and those ultimate questions in life: Who am I? Why am I here? and Where am I going?

We were working in my art studio, sculpting reproductions of old New England gravestones and we realized that there are certain times in our lives when we are more likely to ask those ultimate questions. The first time is when we are in our early twenties—just heading out in life. We are aware of our gifts and talents but they are largely untested. There's anxiety but there's also optimism and idealism. We figure that even if we screw up, there's still time to fix things. But we wonder what our worth is determined by. Is it based on what we produce or how much we can earn or is it based on something else?

A few years pass and suddenly we find ourselves in a midlife crisis, and those haunting questions return. Now we have teenagers, and they're telling us that we're boring and that we need to "get a life." We answer: "I'd like to get a life but I have all these obligations." But we know they're right. We know we're stuck in a mundane rut and there's this hole in us—it's empty and we want to fill it with something. We look back at our lives and we see that we've reached some of our goals but we hold many other dreams that are still unfulfilled. Maybe one of our parents has died and we are painfully aware of our own mortality. For some, a panic sets in and they say, "I will never be young again." We may begin to do stupid things like buy a red sports car or look for joy in the wrong places and all the while, this hole in us is growing and we hear the sad refrain from that U2 song playing over and over again in our heads: "but I still haven't found what I'm looking for . . ."

The next time we consider these questions is when disaster strikes. We lose a loved one or we watch as jetliners slam into the World Trade Center and thousands of people are incinerated within minutes. Church bells ring in New York City and long dormant cathedrals fill up suddenly with people all wondering the same things: Who am I—really? Why am I here—really? Where am I going—really?

I remember just after 9/11 watching a man interviewed on television. He was standing on the streets of New York City, like one who had nowhere to go. He had been an investment broker who had developed a successful business that had been located in one of the Twin Towers—on a floor that had taken a direct hit. He was late for work that day and escaped, but all of his life's work and all of his colleagues were gone. He was just standing there shaking his head saying, "All my life I pursued money and defined myself by the accumulation of wealth and now I see it's meaningless." He then asked "How am I going to define myself now?"

The last time that we ask those ultimate questions is at the end of our own lives. We may have a terminal illness or maybe we are ninety years old and healthy like my mom, but we know that this life doesn't go on forever. Now those haunting questions are rephrased as we ask, Who was I? Why was I here? Where will I be going?

My dad died in 1988. He was a phenomenal artist and received the praise and affirmation of many all his life, and when he died he left some of his best paintings to his family. After the funeral, my mom said to me, "Dad left all these paintings but . . . what am I going to leave?" I answered, "Mom, you nurtured us and adored us. That's worth more than all the paintings in the world."

When I told this to Justin he made a comment. He said, "Sometimes I think we're all just slabs of meat marinating in a culture of emptiness, and it's the kind of emptiness that tells us that the tangible is more valuable than the divine." He knew we were more than that. But he was also struck by the cultural forces that undermined our sense of value and the true origin of it. Even when we are rock solid, even when we are on a strong foundation, we can be consumed at times by self-doubt. During moments like these, we just wonder, Did I matter? I think my mom's question gives voice to one of the deepest longings in our hearts. Does my life have significance? Is there any meaning to it at all? Or is this just a cosmic crap shoot?

As our conversation progressed, Justin and I began to ask what really determines our significance and our value. Is it only based on how well we perform in the classroom, or the boardroom, or the courtroom, or the bedroom? Or is it based on something else, and if so, what? Then I told him about one of the most important experiences of my life involving his sister Emily. It was 1992 and I had just completed fifteen years of successes and was feeling pretty proud of myself. But then I set a moderate goal and failed completely in a very public and humiliating way. I was angry at myself and angry at a few people who had prevented me from reaching that goal. I was *in a deep blue funk for about a year wondering,* What's it all about anyway?

Then one night Emily asked me to tuck her in bed, so I did. She was just three years old then. I read her a story and prayed with her and turned out the light. But she said, "Daddy, will you stay with me for a while until I fall asleep?" So I did. I climbed under the covers and put my head on her pillow—our noses were only inches apart. She was looking at my face but I was being a space cadet. I was wondering, Why does God love any of us? Why does he see us as valuable? What is it? I knew that God wasn't impressed by our performances. It had to be something else. I knew that he cared for the vulnerable, the weak, the afflicted, the widow and the orphan, and people who weren't doing too well. He loved Zacchaeus up in the sycamore tree—even while that tax collector exploited his own people and betrayed his nation for an occupying power. And yet Jesus called him down from the tree and wanted to transform his life.

So why does God do that? I was thinking these thoughts when all of a sudden, Emily called to me: "Daddy, Daddy." Earth to Daddy. Back then, she had the habit of sandwiching my face between her hands when she wanted to get my attention and so she did that and I said, "What, Emmy?" Then she took her two index fingers and stuck them up her nose and said, "Do this." So I stuck my fingers up my nose, which sent her into a giggle fit. But I just looked at her and thought, Wow, do I love this girl! *I thought,* I adore her. I'd do anything for her. I'd go into a burning building. I'd die. I wouldn't want to live without any of my children.

Then suddenly I remembered that Emily wasn't always a very good performer. Just a few days earlier, she had taken a green magic marker with indelible ink and drawn a picture on the brand new wall-to-wall carpet in her bedroom. One week before that, I had parked a new Honda Civic in the driveway and Emmy had taken a stone and scratched a smiley face in the side of the car. But as I was looking at this giggling girl with her fingers up her nose, I thought, I don't care about the carpet and I don't care about the car. What I care about is that I adore her and she adores me and there's this fulfillment that comes from intimacy that beats everything.

It suddenly dawned on me that that's why God values us. That's why God made us. That's why God put us here. It doesn't matter how much we screw up. He wants to adore you and he wants to be adored. That hole in us is going to be empty until we get it—until we understand that there's something that transcends the red sports car or whatever else that we put into our lives to ease the pain. He desires us and once we understand that, suddenly those ultimate questions aren't just questions anymore—they are personal invitations that have been hard-wired into our souls by God himself—inviting us to draw close to the only One who can satisfy us forever.

But as soon as Justin and I considered these things, we both realized that there's a huge problem. The problem is that none of us is three years old anymore and anyone who's spent any length of time in this world has been damaged by it. When that happens, we often choose exile. We choose a fortress. We choose to isolate ourselves. We don't act like happy little three year olds anymore.

Some of the people that Justin loved the dearest were people who had been raised by alcoholics. They had learned at an early age to avoid emotional pain at all costs. They would say, "I'm not damaged. I'm not wounded. I'm actually stronger because of what I've been through." Meanwhile, all their friends saw them as wounded creatures on the jungle floor, fluffing up their feathers and raising the fur on their backs—trying to look bigger than they actually were. Some of them had all the sex they could ever hope to have but they never knew real intimacy because that would mean baring their souls and not just their bodies. But sometimes, out of all that emptiness and misery and solitude and isolation, we hear an iconoclastic voice pleading and calling to us: "What you call safe isn't really safe." And we hear the inaugural words of Jesus saying, "The Spirit of God is upon me to proclaim release to the captives . . . and to set at liberty those who have been bruised."

Justin and I then talked about what that liberty looks like. I heard from one of his friends who told me that when my son was in a pub in

Wyoming, he stood up on a table and began to make fun of himself. He was laughing at his insecurities and inadequacies and he got everyone else laughing. By the time the experience was over with, people thought, "This guy is pretty cool. He's letting down his guard and being real with us and maybe it's safe to do the same with him." Guys became buddies. There was a sense of community and there was grace.

Sometimes I think that we toss God from our lives because we're terrified of the freedom that he offers. It's the freedom to stand up on a table and be real. It's the freedom to go to another person and say, "I'm sorry. I was wrong. Would you forgive me?" It's the freedom to let go of our rage and forgive others. It's the freedom to have that kind of intimacy that we were created for—both with others and with our Maker.

Justin was known for living life to the fullest. I think if he were here today, he would want to say to anyone who is terrified of that freedom, "What could be more terrifying than a life of cowardice? What could be more tragic than knowing that there are loved ones who have desired us their whole lives but never got to have us because we withheld our souls from them—fearful of being fully known?" I think he'd say, "What could be more hopeless than entering eternity trapped in a cage—a cage of our own making, emptied of God, intimacy, and meaning?" I know from numerous conversations with my son that he wanted something more. He was willing to sacrifice himself—sacrifice his ego and be real to get it. He heard the voice of God calling to him: "Come away from that emptiness, my beloved. The mystery and the meaning of suffering are found in the intimacy that it brings." He knew that God offered him a satisfaction of the soul that he could find nowhere else.

I was wondering if we could do something in Justin's honor? You don't have to do it if your heart isn't ready. But tonight, when you are in bed and the lights are out and you're all alone or your spouse is asleep, ask God to sandwich your face between his hands. Give him your full attention. Then take your two index fingers and stick them up your nose and say:

God, here I am in all my glory and all my shame. I'm frightened by this freedom that you offer but I'm tired of running from it. I'm tired of being that wounded creature on the jungle floor. I'm tired of being an expert at avoidance and denial. I'm tired of that broken part in me and I ask that you would heal me and bring me back to the place where I desired intimacy more than the empty promises of this exile.

God, I'm tired of the trappings of religion. I'm tired of taking communion without having communion. I'm tired of that naïve gullibility that's so often associated with kooky beliefs and cultic thinking as if true discipleship has nothing to do with the piercing, analytical, discerning, probing, penetrating mind of God. I'm tired of fig leaves that can't conceal my shame. I'm tired of the fleeting splendor of my accomplishments. I'm tired of scholarship that's defined by moral skepticism and human arrogance. I'm tired of that paralyzing cynicism that could never heal or redeem anyone from anything. I'm willing to be true to my own cynicism by being cynical of even it. I'm willing to peel back all the layers of hurt and shame and resentment and rage to find out what lurks beneath and to ask myself, "Why in the world have I replaced a Fountain of Living Water with a scum-filled bucket that could never quench my thirst?"

I'm tired, God, of being haunted by the same questions that haunt everyone else in this world, and yet I feel so completely alone. I give up. I surrender. I lay down my arms and I take off my masks. I return from my self-imposed exile.

Romance my soul, Lord. Turn my heart to putty and let me melt into the arms of One who has already rushed into a burning building to save his child. God, let me be the kind of person who can walk through life with confidence saying, "I know who I am. I know why I'm here. I know where I'm going. No one is going to shut me down." And when my life is done, let me strap on a set of skis like Justin and outrun the avalanche of this world's emptiness one last time. Let me sail off into eternity knowing that I had the opportunity to draw close to the Lover of my Soul and I took it. I didn't run away in fear, but I finally embraced you, Lord, with complete, joyful abandon.[22]

Endnotes

1. Jefferson Hascall, "Angel Band," 1860.
2. Information on Invisible Children may be found at www.invisiblechildren.com
3. Rainer Maria Rilke, trans. John L. L. Mood, *Rilke on Love and Other Difficulties* (New York: W. W. Norton, 1975), 25.
4. C. S. Lewis, *The Problem of Pain* (San Francisco: HarperSanFrancisco, 2001), 39.
5. C. S. Lewis, *The Problem of Pain*, 41.
6. C. S. Lewis, *The Problem of Pain*, 46.
7. Author's Valentine to his wife.
8. Marianne Schneider Corey and Gerald Corey, *Groups: Process and Practice* (Pacific Grove, Calif. : Brooks Cole Publishing, 1992), 18.
9. Henri Nouwen, *In the Name of Jesus: Reflections on Christian Leadership* (New York: Crossroad, 1992), 59–60.
10. Charles Reade, *A Simpleton* (Seattle: World Wide School, 2001), chap. XIII. http://www.worldwideschool.com/library/books/lit/drama/ASimpleton/chap14.html
11. Czeslaw Milosz, *The Captive Mind*, trans. Jane Zielonko (New York: Vintage Books, 1981), 215.

12 Czeslaw Milosz, *The Captive Mind*, 219.
13 Abraham Joshua Heschel, *The Insecurity of Freedom* (New York: Schocken Books, 1972), back cover.
14 Os Guinness, *Time for Truth: Living Free in a World of Lies, Hype and Spin* (Grand Rapids, Mich. : Baker Books, 2000), 78.
15 Edward N. Lorenz, *The Essence of Chaos* (Seattle: The University of Washington Press, 1995), 159.
16 Abraham J. Heschel, *The Prophets* (New York: Harper & Row, 1969), 191.
17 John Newton, "Amazing Grace," 1772.
18 See Karl Barth, *Church Dogmatics*, IV, 3 (Grand Rapids, Mich. : Eerdmans, 1981), 592.
19 Abraham Joshua Heschel, *The Insecurity of Freedom* (New York: Schocken Books, 1972), 177.
20 Abraham Joshua Heschel, *The Insecurity of Freedom*, 134.
21 George Bennard, "The Old Rugged Cross," 1913.
22 Author's eulogy, delivered at the memorial service for his son Justin Kautz, [February 24, 2007, White River Junction, Vermont]